THE BEST OF LON

MOON LONDON WALKS

Step off the plane and head for the newest, hippest café in town. Discover where to get the best fish and chips in the city or where to find locally brewed beer on tap. In *Moon London Walks*, you'll find inside information on numerous hidden gems. This way, you can skip the busy shopping streets and stroll through the city at your own pace, taking in a local attraction on your way to the latest and greatest shops. Savor every second and make your trip a truly great experience.

LONDON BOUND!

You're about to discover London, one of our favorite cities. The charming neighborhoods, amazing museums, and fabulous galleries are inspiring, and we love all of the shopping possibilities—from big, beautiful department stores to small, independent boutiques. Booking a table at the restaurant of a celebrity chef or cookbook author is pretty cool, too, not to mention the city's many great markets, the view from the London Eye, the old-school boat rides on the Thames, and all the trendy cocktail bars mixing up perfect gin and tonics. Winter, spring, summer, and fall, London buzzes year-round.

ABOUT THIS BOOK

In this book, our local author shares with you the genuine highlights of the city she loves. Discover the city by foot and at your own pace, so you can relax and experience the local lifestyle without having to do a lot of preparation beforehand. That means more time for you. Our walks take you past our favorite restaurants, cafés, museums, galleries, shops, and other notable attractions— places we ourselves like to go to. So who knows, you might even run into us.

None of the places mentioned here has paid to appear in either the text or the photos, and all text has been written by an independent editorial staff.

<u>CITY</u>
LONDON

<u>WORK & ACTIVITIES</u>
MARKETING MANAGER

Kim studied fashion at the Amsterdam Fashion Institute and London College of Fashion. She loves vintage boutiques, pop-up markets, and decadent department stores. Her favorite things to do in London include practicing yoga, playing table tennis, bowling, catching a movie at the secret cinema, and wandering through the city. She also regularly visits the fabulous exhibitions at Tate Modern and the V&A (Victoria and Albert Museum).

<u>LOCAL</u>
KIM SNIJDERS

PRACTICAL INFORMATION

The six walks in this book allow you to discover the funnest neighborhoods in the city by foot and at your own pace. They will take you past museums and notable attractions, but more importantly, they'll show you where to go for good food, drinks, shopping, entertainment, and an overall good time. Check out the map at the front of this book to see which areas of the city the routes will take you through.

Each route is clearly indicated on a detailed map at the beginning of the relevant chapter. The map also specifies where each place mentioned is located. The color of the number lets you know what type of venue it is (see the key at the bottom of this page). A description of each place is then given later in the chapter.

Without taking into consideration extended stops at any one location, each route will take a maximum of three hours. The approximate distance is indicated at the top of the page, before the directions.

PRICES
Next to the address and contact details of each location, we give an idea of how much you can expect to spend there. Unless otherwise stated, the amount given in restaurant listings is the average price of a main course. For sights and attractions, we indicate the cost of a regular full-price ticket.

LEGEND

● >> SIGHTS & ATTRACTIONS   ● >> SHOPPING

● >> FOOD & DRINK   ● >> MORE TO EXPLORE

☼ >> WALK HIGHLIGHT

CITY OF LONDON

GOOD TO KNOW

Most stores in London are open seven days a week, usually from 10am until 8pm with shorter hours on Sunday. There are exceptions, of course, so always make sure to check the opening hours at your destination before you head out. On public holidays, or "bank holidays" as they are called in England, most stores remain open, and public transportation still runs, but expect shorter Sunday hours.

Restaurants often automatically add a 10 to 15 percent gratuity to your bill. Although leaving a tip isn't required, it is customary—but double-check your bill to be sure you don't end up tipping twice. If no gratuity has been added to your check, it's expected that you'll leave about a 10 percent tip.

London has strict smoking laws. Smoking is banned in enclosed public spaces, including hotels, bars, restaurants, theaters, and on public transportation.

Whenever possible, book tickets for the train and any sights and attractions in advance. Online prices are often significantly lower than what you'll pay at the door.

FOOD AND DRINK

A typical English breakfast is the "full English" or "fry-up" and consists of fried eggs, bacon, toast, and baked beans.

In London, as in the rest of England, a relatively elaborate Sunday lunch is a well-established tradition. Known as a Sunday roast, this meal includes meat, potatoes, vegetables, and Yorkshire pudding.

Another great tradition is, of course, afternoon tea, which is not to be confused with high tea. Afternoon tea takes place around 4pm and consists of a combination of sweet and savory bites along with a cup of tea. High tea, on the other hand, is essentially a simple evening meal.

Londoners drink their fair share of tea—preferably strong, black tea with a splash of milk. This popular drink is known here as "builder's tea."

PUBLIC HOLIDAYS

Public holidays are referred to as "bank holidays" in the UK because banks are closed on these days. Many of these bank holidays are on Mondays. In addition to Good Friday and Easter Monday, which don't fall on a specific date, the following are official holidays in the UK:

January 1 > New Year's Day
First Monday in May > May Day Bank Holiday
Last Monday in May > Spring Bank Holiday
Last Monday in August > Summer Bank Holiday
December 25 > Christmas Day
December 26 > Boxing Day

HAVE ANY TIPS?

Shops and restaurants in London come and go fairly regularly. We do our best to keep the walks and contact details as up to date as possible. We also do our best to update the print edition as often as we can. However, if despite our best efforts there is still a place that you can't find or if you have any other comments or tips, please let us know via email at info@momedia.nl.

TRANSPORTATION

The train or bus will get you downtown within 45 minutes from any of London's five **airports.** Expect to pay about £15 each way for the train and about £10 for the bus. A taxi will set you back at least £55. Train information is available at www.thetrainline.com. From Heathrow and London city airports you can take the subway, referred to locally as "the Underground" or "the Tube," into the city for about £4.50.

If you're traveling by **Eurostar** via the Channel Tunnel, you'll arrive at St. Pancras International railway station. From here you can easily take the Tube or bus to any corner of the city.

Once in central London, the fastest way to get around is with the **Underground.** Buy an **Oyster card** for £10 and save on subway, bus, and certain train tickets. The average fare for a Tube ride, for example, costs £4.80 without an Oyster card but just £2.30 with one. You can purchase a prepaid Oyster card online and at most stations. The card is easy to use; just swipe it whenever you enter or leave a station. For more information, check out www.tfl.gov.uk. A map of the London Underground is available in the back of our book.

The **bus** is a great way to see the city. A ride to or from central London costs £1.50 with an Oyster card. The destination is clearly indicated on the front of every bus, together with some of the stops along the way. London also has an extensive network of night buses. See www.tfl.gov.uk/buses for more details.

Thanks to the open **double-decker tour buses,** it's even possible to see a good deal of London's most notable attractions in a couple of hours in one easy loop. Various companies run tours leaving from Victoria Station, Trafalgar Square, Piccadilly, and other popular tourist destinations, but the Original Tour is a good option. Tickets cost £27 online, and there are plenty of hop-on, hop-off stops to choose from. See www.theoriginaltour.com.

INTRODUCTION

Taxis, or "black cabs" as they are called in London, are easy to hail by sticking out your hand. A taxi is available when the top light is on. Taxis offer an affordable way to travel when you're with three or more people and aren't traveling far. Minicabs, or private taxis, are cheaper but aren't always as reliable. You can't just hail a minicab on the street—they need to be booked in advance—and if one randomly stops and offers its services, you'd do best not to take it. Use whatever company your hotel uses instead. Prices should be agreed on beforehand.

You can also get around quickly in London by **boat.** There are many options for water travel, from speedy line services to slow leisure cruises. Find out more at www.tfl.gov.uk/river and www.thamesclippers.com for high-speed boats.

BIKING

Despite the heavy left-hand traffic and the lack of bike lanes, biking is becoming increasingly more popular in London. This is thanks in part to former mayor Boris Johnson, who used to cycle to work himself, launched the city's **bike-share** system, Santander Cycles, and oversaw the creation of multiple-cycle superhighways. Be sure to stay alert while riding because cars and buses don't always look out for cyclists—they're not used to them, and cyclists are often a source of frustration. Helmets are not required but are recommended. Also note that, unlike in other parts of Europe, it's uncommon to park your bike on the side of the road in London.

Renting a bike in London can be great fun. Walks 5 and 6 through Marylebone, Regent's Park & Primrose Hill, and Knightsbridge & Chelsea are particularly well suited for cycling. Rent a Santander Cycle, locally referred to as a "Boris bike." These bikes are available around the city and are easy to rent from a docking station using a credit card. Rates start at £2 per day. The first half hour is free, and each additional half hour costs £2. Visit www.tfl.gov.uk/cycling for more information and nice bike routes.

TOP 10	RESTAURANTS

1 Kick-start your day at **The Good Life Eatery** > p. 105

2 Order a mouth-watering Sunday roast at **The Engineer** > p. 110

3 Go for brunch at the charming **German Gymnasium** > p. 85

4 Indulge in a Mediterranean meal at **Ottolenghi** > p. 90

5 Enjoy vegetarian and vegan fare at **Mildreds** > p. 89

6 Try British classics with a modern twist at **Lyle's** > p. 66

7 Eat a traditional Sunday roast at **Roast** > p. 49

8 **Momo** serves up delicious North African dishes in a lively atmosphere > p. 30

9 Dine in style at the up-scale **Mews of Mayfair** > p. 30

10 Come to **Kin** for affordable Asian food > p. 50

TOP 10	SUNDAYS

1 Start the day with breakfast at **The Modern Pantry** > p. 50

2 Learn about science at the **Science Museum** > p. 122

3 Take a walk, ride a bike, fly a kite, or have a picnic in **Regent's Park** > p. 98

4 Shop at **Liberty,** one of London's best-loved department stores > p. 34

5 See the gorillas and other animals at the **London Zoo** > p. 117

6 Visit the Queen at **Buckingham Palace** > p. 18

7 Enjoy afternoon tea at **The Berkeley Hotel** > p. 129

8 Board the **London Eye** for the best views of the city > p. 37

9 Bask in the botanical splendor at **Kew Gardens** > p. 138

10 Order fish & chips at **The Golden Hind** > p. 105

1 Shop for antiques at **Alfies Antique Market** > p. 114

2 Enjoy the vibe the tasty snacks at **Borough Market** > p. 57

3 Discover unique, handmade products and great food at **Sunday Upmarket** > p. 76

4 Check out the famous **Portobello Road Market** > p. 138

5 See the bustling and colorful **Columbia Road Flower Market** > p. 77

6 Mix with London's hippest at **Broadway Market** > p. 142

7 **Smithfield Market** is famous for its meat > p. 57

8 Sample the street food at **Maltby Street Market** > p. 46

9 Pick up nice vintage items at **Spitalfields Market** > p. 76

10 **Partridges Food Market** is crammed with food trucks > p. 129

TOP 10 — NIGHTLIFE

1 Enjoy a night at **House of Burlesque** > 27 Old Gloucester Street

2 Mingle with hipsters at **Café OTO** > 18-22 Ashwin Street

3 Enjoy a drink at **Oslo** > 1a Armhurst Road

4 **Union Chapel** is a great music venue > Compton Terrace

5 The **Cahoots** bar is an old air raid shelter > 13 Kingly Court

6 **Queen of Hoxton** is a bar and gallery > 1-5 Curtain Road

7 **Bounce** has table tennis, food, and drinks > 121 Holborn

8 Every night is different at **93 Feet East** > 150 Brick Lan

9 **Happiness Forgets** is an intimate setting > 8-9 Hoxton Square.

10 Party at the glamorous **Proud Embankment** > 8 Victoria Embankment

WESTMINSTER, ST. JAMES'S & MAYFAIR

ABOUT THE WALK

This walk takes you past all of the sights London is most famous for. Much of the focus is on history and culture, but there are also plenty of good shopping opportunities along the way, as well as up-scale restaurants and hotels where you can enjoy a nice dinner or afternoon tea. The route is fairly long, so consider cycling the middle section through St. James's Park if you want to save time.

THE NEIGHBORHOODS

Westminster lies on the north bank of the River Thames and is the iconic London featured on postcards. Numerous places in Westminster are included on UNESCO's World Heritage list, and the area is incredibly popular among tourists. Since as early as the 11th century, Great Britain has been ruled from this corner of London. Westminster is home to political and religious power hubs such as the **Houses of Parliament, 10 Downing Street,** and **Westminster Abbey.** The most famous part of the Houses of Parliament is the bell tower and clock referred to as Big Ben. The Palace of Westminster that is home to the Parliament was originally built in the 11th century. However, due to a fire in 1834, most of the current structure dates to around 1840. South of Westminster you'll find **St. James's Park** and **Buckingham Palace,** the top royal attraction in the city. Ever since Queen Victoria made it her home in 1837, Buckingham Palace has been the official residence of the British monarchy. Today the Queen is nearly the sole resident of this part of London—the stately buildings in this area are primarily home to up-scale businesses, government offices, and ultra-expensive, unoccupied apartments.

North of St. James's Park lie the posh neighborhoods **St. James's** and **Mayfair.** In addition to the beautiful historical buildings and elegant squares here, these neighborhoods are known for their social clubs (traditional gentlemen's clubs) and

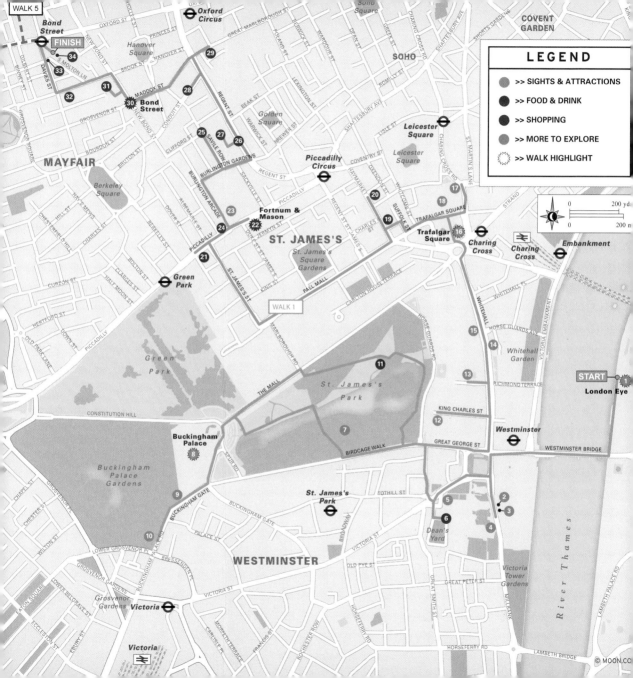

WALK 5

Bond
Street
FINISH

Oxford
Circus

SOHO

COVENT
GARDEN

LEGEND

>> SIGHTS & ATTRACTIONS

>> FOOD & DRINK

>> SHOPPING

>> MORE TO EXPLORE

>> WALK HIGHLIGHT

Hanover
Square

Soho
Square

29

34
33
32
31
30 Bond
Street

28

27
26
25

24

23

22

21

Leicester
Square

Leicester
Square

MAYFAIR

Berkeley
Square

Golden
Square

Piccadilly
Circus

20

18

17

19

Trafalgar
Square

Trafalgar
Square

16

Charing
Cross

Charing
Cross

Embankment

0   200 yds
0   200 m

ST. JAMES'S

Fortnum &
Mason

St. James's
Square
Gardens

Charing
Cross

Charing
Cross

Embankment

Green
Park

WALK 1

PALL MALL

CARLTON HOUSE TERRACE

WHITEHALL PL.

15

14

Whitehall
Garden

13

START

London Eye

Green
Park

St. James's
Park

11

Westminster

12

Buckingham
Palace

8

7

King Charles St

GREAT GEORGE ST

Westminster

WESTMINSTER BRIDGE

Buckingham
Palace
Gardens

9

BIRDCAGE WALK

St. James's
Park

10

5

2
3

6

4

Dean's
Yard

River Thames

WESTMINSTER

Victoria
Tower
Gardens

Grosvenor
Gardens

Victoria

Victoria

© MOON.CO

perfectly tailored suits. Since 1800 **Savile Row** has been one of the best-known streets for tailor-made clothing and custom-made shoes. **Bond Street** and New Bond Street in Mayfair are also home to the shops of famous high-end fashion brands. The luxury boutiques, jewelry shops, and antique stores are a shopping paradise for those with an accommodating wallet. In St. James's and Mayfair, you'll also find a number of famous art institutions and auction houses, including the **Royal Academy,** Christie's, and Sotheby's.

SHORT ON TIME? HERE ARE THE HIGHLIGHTS:
1 LONDON EYE + 8 BUCKINGHAM PALACE + 16 TRAFALGAR SQUARE + 22 AFTERNOON TEA AT FORTNUM & MASON + 30 BOND STREET

TIPS
// Ideal for first-time visitors
// This long route is suitable for biking
// The many sights and attractions make this a great walk for a Sunday

WALK 1 DESCRIPTION (approx. 7 mi/11 km)

Start with the view from the London Eye ❶. Take Westminster Bridge across the Thames and go left to the Houses of Parliament ❷ ❸. Across the street is the Jewel Tower ❹. Walk back, turn left at Parliament Square, take Broad Sanctuary, and go left on Victoria Street to Westminster Abbey ❺ ❻. Cross the street and take Storey's Gate to St. James's Park ❼. Go left to Buckingham Palace ❽—you can't miss it. The Queen's Gallery ❾ and the Royal Mews ❿ are behind the palace. Walk back through St. James's Park, a great place to sit down and take a break ⓫, to Parliament Square. Turn left on Parliament Street. The Churchill War Rooms ⓬ are on the first street to the left. Parliament Street turns into Whitehall, which takes you past Downing Street ⓭, Banqueting House ⓮, and Horse Guards ⓯. At the end of Whitehall is Trafalgar Square ⓰ ⓱ ⓲. Cross Trafalgar Square, go left on Pall Mall, right on Suffolk Street, then take the first street to the left for a drink or meal in a colorful setting ⓳. Continue to Dover Street Market ⓴. Back on Pall Mall, follow the road to St. James's Street, then turn left on Piccadilly to The Wolseley ㉑. Walk back to Piccadilly and turn left to Fortnum & Mason ㉒ and the Royal Academy ㉓. Backtrack a bit on Piccadilly, turn right and walk through Burlington Arcade ㉔. Exit at the other end, then turn right, walk past Savile Row ㉕, and take Vigo Street to Regent Street ㉖. Turn left. The first street on the left, Heddon Street, leads to a square where you'll find Momo ㉗. Continue on Regent Street and turn left for Sketch ㉘. Head back on Regent Street and turn right on Great Marlborough Street to Liberty department store ㉙. Then turn left and head down Maddox Street. Continue on Maddox Street to New Bond Street ㉚ and turn right. Go left down an alley more or less across from Armani to Mews of Mayfair ㉛. Then go back to Bond Street, continue to Brook Street and turn left for the best afternoon tea in London ㉜. Cross and take Davies Street to Grays Antiques ㉝ and the charming shops of South Molton Street ㉞. This is where the high-end fun stops and puts you on Oxford Street, Europe's biggest shopping street.

SIGHTS & ATTRACTIONS

❷ The Palace of Westminster, better known as the **Houses of Parliament,** is a labyrinth of more than 1,000 stately rooms in which the British government conducts its routine business. The most famous part of the palace is the giant bell tower and clock commonly referred to as Big Ben. The palace was originally built in the late 11th century; however, due to a fire in 1834, most of the current structure dates to around 1840. Tours of the palace are possible during parliament's summer recess, and reservations are required. It is also possible to attend a debate.

Parliament Square, www.parliament.uk, open see website for more information, tour £25, Tube Westminster

❹ The **Jewel Tower** is one of the few remaining parts of the original medieval palace that now forms the Houses of Parliament. At the time, the tower was built as a place to store the king's jewels and treasures. Today it houses an exhibition on the history of the British parliament.

Parliament Square, www.english-heritage.org.uk, tel. 0370 333 1181, see website for more information, entrance £5.40, Tube Westminster

❺ The beautiful Gothic church **Westminster Abbey**—where Prince William and Kate Middleton were married—is something of a covered graveyard. For the past thousand years, many famous kings and queens have been buried here, along with numerous poets, scientists, musicians, and soldiers. Services here are open to the public.

20 Deans Yard, www.westminster-abbey.org, tel. 020 7222 5152, Mon-Tue & Thur-Fri 9:30am-3:30pm, Wed 9:30am-6pm, Sat 9:30am-2:30pm, entrance £20, Tube Westminster/St. James's Park

⚙ Ever since Queen Victoria made it her home in 1837, **Buckingham Palace** has been the official residence of the British monarchy. In August and September, only some of the palace's 775 rooms are open to the public. Most visitors, however, come here to see the Changing of the Guard.

St. James's Park, www.royalcollection.org.uk, tel. 020 7766 7300, Changing of the Guard April-Aug daily 11:30am, Sept-March odd days 11:30am, Changing of the Guard free, entrance to Royal State Rooms £24, Tube Victoria/Green Park/Hyde Park Corner

9 Until recently, the Queen's enormous art collection, the Royal Collection, was not open to the public. Today, however, this great collection is no longer kept hidden. At the **Queen's Gallery** you can see important pieces from the collection by artists such as Michelangelo, Vermeer, and Rubens.
Buckingham Palace, St. James's Park, www.royalcollection.org.uk, tel. 020 7766 7301, open daily 10am-5:30pm, Jul 31-Sep 30 9:30am-5:30pm, entrance £12, Tube Victoria/Green Park/Hyde Park Corner

10 Curious about the royal family's horses, carriages, and motor vehicles? You can see them for yourself at the **Royal Mews.** Among other things, here you'll find the Gold State Coach, which was built in 1762 for King George III.
Buckingham Palace, Buckingham Palace Road, www.royalcollection.org.uk, tel. 020 7766 7302, open daily Feb-Mar & Nov 10am-4pm, Apr-Oct 10am-5pm, closed during State visits, entrance £11, Tube Victoria

12 During World War II, Churchill directed numerous military operations from within the subterranean **Churchill War Rooms.** The underground complex remains virtually unchanged today and gives an excellent glimpse into life in wartime London. Visit the adjoining Churchill Museum to discover the story of Winston Churchill's life.
King Charles Street, www.iwm.org.uk/visits/churchill-war-rooms, tel. 020 7416 5000, open daily 9:30am-6pm, entrance £18.90, Tube Westminster/St. James's Park

13 London's best-known address, **10 Downing Street,** has been the home and office of the British prime minister since 1732. Many a famous foot has crossed the threshold of this notable building. Unfortunately, most of us will have to settle for a peek of the famous front door from the other side of a fence, although a virtual tour is available online.
10 Downing Street, www.number10.gov.uk, Tube Westminster/St. James's Park

14 **Banqueting House** is the only remaining building from the original Whitehall Palace, which burned down in 1689. Among other things, check out the amazing ceiling painting by Rubens that dates back to 1629. Fantastic classical concerts are also organized here.
Whitehall, www.hrp.org.uk/banquetinghouse, tel. 084 4482 7777, open daily 10am-5pm, entrance £5.50, Tube Westminster/Embankment/Charing Cross

⑮ **Horse Guards** is the official entrance to the royal palaces. Guards—both on horseback and on foot—don't appear to be keeping an eye on anything in particular. Mainly they stoically ignore the many tourists here. The Changing of the Guard at Horse Guards also takes place with the necessary pomp and ceremony.
Whitehall, www.royal.gov.uk, open Changing of the Guard Mon-Sat 11am, Sun 10am, free, Tube Westminster/St. James's Park/Embankment

⑯ **Trafalgar Square** is London's central square. People come here to protest, ring in the New Year, and celebrate Eid-al-Fitr, Diwali, the Chinese New Year, and much more. This is also a place people come to just hang out or, when the weather is warm, cool off in the fountains. Nearly every weekend there is some event going on here.
Trafalgar Square, www.london.gov.uk/trafalgarsquare, Tube Charing Cross

⑰ With tens of thousands of portraits, the **National Portrait Gallery** provides a good overview of British history from the 16th century to the present. Nearly anyone who has meant anything in the UK is represented here in a painting, photo, or sculpture—from Shakespeare to Kate Moss and David Bowie. The restaurant on the top floor offers a fantastic view and delicious food.
St. Martin's Place, www.npg.org.uk, tel. 020 7306 0055, open Mon-Wed & Sat-Sun 10am-6pm, Thur-Fri 10am-9pm, free, Tube Charing Cross/Leicester Square/Embankment

⑱ Unless you have several days to spend at the **National Gallery,** you'll have to make some serious choices here because you won't be able to see everything. The museum houses the national collection of Western European art from the 13th to early 20th centuries and includes works from Van Gogh, Monet, Seurat, Constable, and Turner.
Trafalgar Square, www.nationalgallery.org.uk, tel. 020 7747 2885, open Mon-Thur & Sat-Sun 10am-6pm, Fri 10am-9pm, free, Tube Charing Cross/Leicester Square

㉓The **Royal Academy** was Britain's first official art school and is primarily known for its temporary exhibitions. The Summer Exhibition, which showcases artwork from both established and emerging artists alike, is especially popular.
Burlington House, Piccadilly, www.royalacademy.org.uk, tel. 020 7300 8000, open daily 10am-6pm, entrance £10, Tube Green Park/Piccadilly Circus

FOOD & DRINK

6 In one of the ancient cellars of Westminster Abbey sits **Cellarium Café & Terrace.** This charming restaurant is a nice spot for breakfast or lunch. Or try the afternoon tea, which includes sweet and savory scones and a selection of delicious cakes. When the weather is nice, the terrace is great too.
20 Dean's Yard, www.cellariumcafe.com, tel. 020 7222 0516, open Mon-Fri 8am-6pm, Sat 9am-5pm, Sun 10am-4pm, price £8, afternoon tea £19, Tube Westminster/St. James's Park

11 **St. James's Cafe** is a gorgeous glass-and-wood structure in the middle of St. James's Park. Sit among the greenery and enjoy the view of the lake. This is an excellent spot for breakfast or lunch. Or stop by later on in the day for drinks.
St. James's Park, https://www.benugo.com/partnerships/public-spaces/parks/st-jamess, open daily 8am-5pm, £7, Tube St. James's Park/Green Park/Charing Cross

19 The upscale Haymarket Hotel is more than just a place to sleep; it also has a great bar and restaurant where you can go for a nice drink or meal. **Brumus** is characterized by the same colorful style the rest of the hotel is known for and does a fabulous afternoon tea.
1 Suffolk Place, www.firmdale.com, tel. 020 7470 4007, open Mon-Sat 7am-11:30pm, Sun 8am-10:30pm, afternoon tea starts at £24, Tube Leicester Square/Piccadilly Circus

21 Breakfast has taken on something of a cult status in London. This can in large part be attributed to the epic breakfast menu at **The Wolseley,** which ranges from a simple pink grapefruit to an extravagant caviar omelet. Of course, you can also opt for something more standard such as regular scrambled eggs. The Wolseley is located in a former Bentley showroom and is the perfect spot to dine in style at any moment of the day.
160 Piccadilly, www.thewolseley.com, tel. 020 7499 6996, open Mon-Fri 7am-midnight, Sat 8am-midnight, Sun 8am-11pm, breakfast £10, Tube Green Park

27 Night after night **Momo** is usually fully booked. The cocktails here are incredibly popular, as is the delicious North African food and lively atmosphere. The weekend brunch here is also stellar. The restaurant is a vibrant oasis hidden just behind the bustling Regent Street.

25 Heddon Street, www.momoresto.com, tel. 020 7434 4040, open Mon-Sat noon-1am, Sun 11am-midnight, from £25, Tube Piccadilly Circus/Oxford Circus

28 Momo's Mourad Mazouz has brought dining in London to a whole new level with **Sketch.** Afternoon tea in the Parlour includes bite-size edible treasures served on funky dishes. The Gallery is an ultra-hip monochromatic space where you can enjoy delicious modern fare. Then there's also the upscale Lecture Room & Library, which has two Michelin stars, and the East Bar, which is a great place for a drink. Whichever you choose here, you are in for an unforgettable night out, guaranteed.

9 Conduit Street, www.sketch.uk.com, tel. 020 7659 4500, Mon-Fri 7am-2am, Sat 8am-2am, Sun 8am-12:30am, from £15, Tube Oxford Circus

31 **Mews of Mayfair** is a stylish restaurant hidden away in a small alley off the bustling New Bond Street. Start with a drink at the cocktail bar on the ground floor. Then head upstairs to the brasserie, where you can enjoy nice seafood or steak. Finally, top it all off with a relaxing after-dinner drink in the sophisticated basement lounge.

10-11 Lancashire Court, New Bond Street, www.mewsofmayfair.com, tel. 020 7518 9388, open Mon-Sat noon-1am, from £20, Tube Bond Street/Oxford Circus

32 Afternoon tea in the Art Deco **Claridge's** hotel is an experience like no other. The live piano and violin music, jacket-clad waitstaff, clinking silver, signature China, extensive tea selection, and delicate pastries and finger sandwiches make Claridge's the number-one place to go for a fancy afternoon tea. Reservations are required and a jacket and tie recommended.

Brook Street, www.claridges.co.uk, tel. 020 7629 8860, afternoon tea daily 2:45pm, 3pm, 3:15pm, 3:30pm, 4:45pm, 5pm, 5:15pm, and 5:30pm, afternoon tea £60, Tube Bond Street

SHOPPING

20 Design Rei Kawakubo of Comme des Garçons created an entirely new type of store with **Dover Street Market.** Not actually a market at all, this one-of-a-kind department store is London's number-one destination for cutting-edge fashion. When you need a break from shopping, head up to Rose Bakery on the top floor—the carrot cake is phenomenal!
18-22 Haymarket, www.doverstreetmarket.com, tel. 020 7518 0680, open Mon-Sat 11am-7pm, Sun noon-6pm, Tube Green Park

22 At the **Fortnum & Mason** department store you can literally get a taste of old England. You could easily fill suitcases with all of the amazing specialty foods here, or have a beautiful "hamper" (gift basket) sent home for your arrival. There are also numerous restaurants at Fortnum's, including the Diamond Jubilee Tea Salon where they offer an amazing afternoon tea. Don't forget to also check out the gorgeous window displays, which are especially fabulous around Christmastime.
181 Piccadilly, www.fortnumandmason.com, tel. 020 7734 8040, open Mon-Sat 10am-9pm, Sun noon-6pm, Tube Green Park/Piccadilly Circus

24 Burlington Arcade is the original upscale shopping mall, which dates back to the 19th century. Today it is home to shops such as Penhaligon's, where you can get fragrant perfumes, and Ladurée, which is known for delicious French macarons. While shopping, be sure to look overhead and take in the gorgeous architecture. Also, watch out for the beadles—these officers, who have been patrolling the arcade since 1819, are part of the old-school charm here, and they won't hesitate to stop you if they catch you running, whistling, or chewing gum.
51 Piccadilly, www.burlington-arcade.co.uk, tel. 020 7493 1764, open Mon-Sat 9am-7:30pm, Sun 11am-6pm, Tube Green Park/Piccadilly Circus

㉕ Both Jermyn Street and **Savile Row** are famous for bespoke tailoring for men. The latter is less old-fashioned but certainly not less pricey. If you're looking for the same quality and don't have the same budget, you can also go to Cad & the Dandy.

Savile Row, open Mon-Sat 10am-6pm, Tube Oxford Circus/Piccadilly Circus

㉖ **Regent Street** is a charming, distinctive London shopping street, and Hamleys, Burberry, and & Other Stories, in particular, deserve special notice. Hamleys is a giant toy store, Burberry is an English classic and home to the original British trench coat. Other Stories is H&M's trendy sister store where you'll find an amazing and affordable collection of clothes, accessories, and cosmetics.

Regent Street, www.regentstreetonline.com, open daily, Tube Oxford Circus/
Piccadilly Circus

㉙ **Liberty** is many Londoners' favorite department store, not only because of the great selection here, but also thanks to the atmosphere and the amazing Tudor-style building that dates from 1924 and was built with the wood of two warships. Here you'll find everything under one roof, including clothes, accessories, cosmetics, furniture, office supplies, and the famous Liberty fabrics.

Regent Street, www.liberty.co.uk, tel. 020 7734 1234, open Mon-Sat 10am-8pm, Sun noon-6pm, Tube Oxford Circus

㉚ Old and New **Bond Street** are the number-one shopping streets for big name junkies. Burberry, Mulberry, Nicole Farhi, Chanel, Louis Vuitton, Gucci, and Prada all have gorgeous shops here. During the January and July sales, prices can drop more than half. Of course, when that happens, everything is so last season.

Old and New Bond Street, www.bondstreetassociation.com, open Mon-Sat 10am-7pm, Sun noon-6pm, Tube Bond Street/Oxford Circus

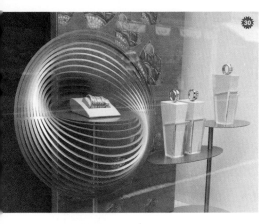

33 Those who love antiques, ceramics, silver, vintage fashion, gems, and jewelry will be able to spend hours wandering through the covered labyrinth that is **Grays Antique Market.** More than 200 vendors spread out over two buildings—Grays and the Mews—come here to sell their wares.
58 Davies Street & 1-7 Davies Mews, www.graysantiques.com, tel. 020 7629 7034, open Mon-Fri 10am-6pm, Sat 11am-5pm, Tube Bond Street

34 Hidden behind the busy Oxford Street lies **South Molton Street.** In this charming shopping area you'll find a nice mix of jewelry, clothing, and shoe stores. European brands such as Sandro, Reiss, Kooples, Kurt Geiger, and Petit Bateau all have stores here.
South Molton Street, open daily, Tube Bond Street

MORE TO EXPLORE

When the **London Eye,** also known as the Millennium Wheel, opened on December 31, 1999, it was the largest Ferris wheel in the world. It is still the tallest in Europe and the most popular paid tourist attraction in the United Kingdom. A ride lasts about half an hour and will carry you up to 443 feet in the air. On clear days, the view over London and far out into the surrounding area is breathtaking. Be sure to book tickets in advance if you don't want to stand in line. It's also less expensive.

South Bank, www.londoneye.com, tel. 087 1781 3000, open daily, tickets start at £23, Tube Westminster/Waterloo

Experience British politics during Question Time in the **House of Commons.** It's a lively sight that often culminates in political theater. Only UK residents can reserve tickets ahead of time; tourists have to wait and see if there are any places left over. The lines for Question Time can be very long, but they often move quickly for other debates.

Houses of Parliament, Parliament Square, www.parliament.uk, tel. 020 7219 4272, open Mon 2:30pm-10:30pm, Tue-Wed 11:30am-7:30pm, Thur 9:30am-5:30pm, Fri 9:30am-3pm, free, Tube Westminster

One of London's most beautiful parks is **St. James's Park.** Here you can rent deck chairs, hang out, and enjoy the fantastic view of Buckingham Palace. Bring some nuts to feed the squirrels and enjoy watching the pelicans swimming around.

St. James's Park, www.royalparks.org.uk, tel. 030 0061 2000, open daily 5am-midnight, free, Tube St. James's Park/Westminster

WALK **2**

SOUTHWARK

ABOUT THE WALK

This varied walk takes you past historical attractions, such as Tower Bridge,
City Hall, and St. Paul's Cathedral. There is a lot of focus on history and culture
on this walk, so you'll also come across great museums such as Tate Modern
and the Design Museum. In Clerkenwell, there are plenty of restaurants,
gastropubs, and charming cafés where you can get a nice bite to eat.

THE NEIGHBORHOODS

South of the Thames lies **Southwark.** Compared to the north side of London,
this side is somewhat underappreciated. Here posh London gives way to a raw,
industrial vibe with warehouses and old train overpasses. The further south you
go, the shabbier the streets are. However, there are still plenty of amazing
things to see in Southwark, including the **Tower, Tower Bridge, Tate Modern,
City Hall,** and **Southwark Cathedral.** In the 16th century London's first
theaters appeared in this neighborhood, including the **Globe,** where
Shakespeare's first performances were held. To this day the reconstructed
theater is a popular attraction. The old **Borough Market,** also on the south side
of the Thames, is an absolute must for anyone who loves food.

Directly across the water stands another London icon: **St. Paul's Cathedral.**
It is surrounded by "the City," London's financial center—also called the Square
Mile. This is the commercial pulse of London and is home to many banks and
offices.

Further to the north you'll find Clerkenwell, a historical neighborhood in the
center of the city. During the 12th century, this neighborhood was home to
many monasteries. However, during the Industrial Revolution the area was built
up, and Clerkenwell transformed into a neighborhood full of factories and
storehouses. The primary residents were blue-collar workers and immigrants,

and for a long time the area had a gritty reputation. In the 1980s it began to be revived, and the warehouses and historical buildings were renovated. Media companies moved in en masse, and the area's image changed. Clerkenwell is now a trendy, creative neighborhood known especially for all its fantastic restaurants. Around Farringdon and Exmouth Market, in particular, there are many good restaurants and gastropubs.

SHORT ON TIME? HERE ARE THE HIGHLIGHTS:

⑤ TOWER BRIDGE + ⑪ BOROUGH MARKET + ⑱ TATE MODERN + ㉒ BARBICAN CENTRE + ㊱ SWEET

TIPS
// Great for first-timers and experienced visitors alike
// The markets and restaurants make this route perfect for foodies
// Not suitable for biking due to traffic

CITY OF LONDON

SOUTHWARK

① Leadenhall Market
② Sky Garden
③ Tower of London
④ St. Katharine Docks
⑤ **Tower Bridge**
⑥ Butler's Wharf
⑦ Maltby Street Market
⑧ Fashion and Textile Museum
⑨ City Hall
⑩ Southwark Cathedral
⑪ **Borough Market**
⑫ Arabica Bar & Kitchen
⑬ Wright Brothers Borough Market
⑭ Roast
⑮ Monmouth Coffee
⑯ Neal's Yard Dairy
⑰ Shakespeare's Globe Theatre
⑱ **Tate Modern**
⑲ Millennium Bridge
⑳ St. Paul's Cathedral
㉑ Museum of London
㉒ **Barbican Centre**
㉓ St. Bartholomew the Great
㉔ Old Red Cow
㉕ Smithfield Market
㉖ Polpo Smithfield
㉗ Hix Oyster & Chop House
㉘ J+A Café
㉙ The Modern Pantry
㉚ Kin
㉛ Magma Bookshop
㉜ Caravan
㉝ Moro
㉞ Space
㉟ Marby & Elm
㊱ **Sweet**

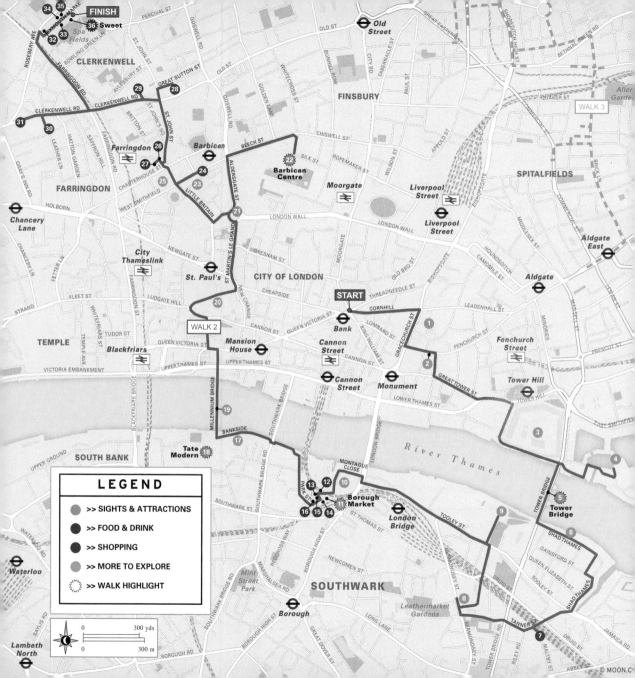

WALK 2 DESCRIPTION (approx. 8.5 mi/13.5 km)

From the Bank Tube station walk down Cornhill and Gracechurch Street to Leadenhall Market ❶, then turn left on Fenchurch Street for the Sky Garden ❷. From there take Rood Lane and Eastcheap to the Tower of London ❸. Then go under the road to get to St. Katharine Docks ❹. Walk back and take the stairs up to Tower Bridge ❺. Once across the river head left to Butler's Wharf ❻. Walk to Maguire Street, then turn left on Gainsford Street. Continue on Shad Thames, which leads onto Tanner Street. Walk under the overpass, then make an immediate left to Maltby Street Market ❼. Walk back to Tanner Street and turn left to continue in the direction you were going until you reach Bermondsey Street, then turn right to visit the Fashion and Textile Museum ❽. Backtrack a short distance and take White's Grounds back under the road to Druid Street, then take that to Tooley Street and turn left. You should now see what appears to be some sort of giant egg: City Hall ❾. Continue to the end of Tooley Street, then go left around Southwark Cathedral ❿ to end up at Borough Market ⓫. In and around the market there are plenty of places to enjoy a cup of coffee or a bite to eat ⓬ ⓭ ⓮ ⓯ ⓰. Next, take Park Street to the Thames and walk along the water to Shakespeare's Globe Theatre ⓱. Further up is the Tate Modern ⓲. Cross back over the river on the Millennium Bridge ⓳, then walk via Queen Victoria Street to Godliman Street to get to St. Paul's Cathedral ⓴. From there take the streets New Change and Cheapside to St. Martin's-Le-Grand and on to the Museum of London ㉑. Continue straight on Aldersgate Street, then right on Beech Street and right again on Silk Street where you'll find the Barbican Centre ㉒. Retrace your steps back to the Museum of London. Make a right on Montague Street and right again on Little Britain to visit the church of St. Bartholomew the Great ㉓. Another right will take you to The Old Red Cow ㉔ and straight ahead is the Smithfield Market ㉕, specializing in wholesale meat. On the other side of the market, take Cowcross Street to the left for something to eat ㉖ ㉗. Otherwise go straight on St. John Street and right on Great Sutton Street to J+A Café ㉘, tucked away on the right. Double back a bit, then turn right on Clerkenwell Road for a bite to eat on St. John's Square ㉙. Continue on Clerkenwell Road and turn left on Leather Lane for some Asian fare ㉚ or straight ahead to Magma Bookshop ㉛. Then walk back the way you came and turn left on Farringdon Road. Continue straight until you get to Rosebury Avenue, then turn right to get to Exmouth Market, where there's no shortage of places to go for a drink, dinner, or more shopping ㉜ ㉝ ㉞ ㉟ ㊱.

SIGHTS & ATTRACTIONS

In 1066 William the Conqueror commissioned the construction of the **Tower of London,** one of the last medieval castles in the world and the site of murders, executions, conspiracy, and betrayal. Discover its history and admire the extensive collection of crown jewels. Be sure to catch one of the free tours led by the Tower's Beefeaters—they are sensational storytellers with vivid tales of the Tower's bloody history. During school holidays, you may even encounter dueling knights, making it feel almost as if you just landed in the middle of a Monty Python sketch.

Tower Hill, www.hrp.org.uk/toweroflondon, tel. 020 3166 6000, open Mar-Oct Sun-Mon 10am-5:30pm, Tue-Sat 9am-5:30 pm, Nov-Feb Sun-Mon 10am-4:30pm, Tue-Sat 9am-4:30pm, entrance £26.80, Tube Tower Hill

When **Tower Bridge** opened in 1894, the steel-framed design was revolutionary. Now, together with Big Ben, it is one of London's most iconic structures, not to mention one of the most famous bridges in the world. Inside you can check out the Tower Bridge Exhibition, visit the Engine Rooms, and traverse the high-level walkway. Since 2014 the view from the walkway has been even more amazing because now there is a glass panel in the floor that lets you look down and see what's going on 138 feet below.

Tower Hill, www.towerbridge.org.uk, tel. 020 7403 3761, open daily Apr-Sep 10am-5:30pm, Oct-Mar 9:30am-5pm, entrance £9.80, Tube Tower Hill

The building that houses the **Fashion and Textile Museum** is hard to miss. With its outrageous color scheme of hot pink, burnt orange, yellow, and bright blue, the converted warehouse has become a tourist attraction in its own right. The museum was founded by the English fashion designer Zandra Rhodes and has regular exhibitions on fashion, textiles, and jewelry.

83 Bermondsey Street, www.ftmlondon.org, tel. 020 7407 8664, open Tue-Sat 11am-6pm, Thur 11am-8pm, Sun 11am-5pm, entrance £8.80, Tube London Bridge

In 2002 the mayor of London got a brand-new office: **City Hall.** It is an impressive glass structure referred to by the locals as the "leaning tower of pizzas" because of the tilted egg-like shape. At City Hall you can visit council

chambers and enjoy the amazing view. In front of the building you'll find the Scoop, an open-air amphitheater with free music and theater performances in the summer.

The Queen's Walk, www.london.gov.uk/city-hall, tel. 020 7983 4000, open Mon-Thur 8:30am-6pm, Fri 8:30am-5:30pm, free, Tube London Bridge

⑩ Southwark Cathedral was built during the 13th century, and it's nothing short of a miracle that England's oldest cathedral still stands today—next to a busy bridge and railroad tracks. Several times each week you can hear beautiful choral music and there are daily masses. The churchyard is a wonderful place to sit and relax.

London Bridge, cathedral.southwark.anglican.org, tel. 020 7367 6700, open Mon-Fri 9am-5pm, Sat 9:30am-3:45pm & 5pm-6pm, Sun 12:30pm-3pm & 4pm-6pm, free, Tour £5, Tube London Bridge

⑱ Works from most of the best-known artists from the 20th century are exhibited in the **Tate Modern,** London's museum of modern art. The impressive building—previously a power plant—is worth a visit. A large-scale installation by a different artist is on display every year in Turbine Hall. The restaurant on the top floor is a welcome respite with a grand view out over the Thames. Be sure to check out the museum store.

Bankside, www.tate.org.uk, tel. 020 7887 8888, open Sun-Thur 10am-6pm, Fri-Sat 10am-10pm, free, prices vary for special exhibitions, Tube Southwark/St. Paul's/Mansion House

⑲ The first pedestrian bridge over the Thames, the **Millennium Bridge,** closed just three days after it opened in 2000 because it began to shake when too many people were on it. That earned it the nickname "the Wobbly Bridge." Since then, the problem has been fixed, and the bridge now offers the perfect way to cross between Tate Modern and St. Paul's Cathedral.

Tube Southwark/St. Paul's

⑳ With an enormous dome, **St. Paul's Cathedral** really stands out in the city. The cathedral, where Prince Charles and Lady Diana Spencer were married, was designed by British scientist and architect Christopher Wren and was built in the late 17th century. Climb the 521 steps for a beautiful view of London.

St. Paul's Churchyard, www.stpauls.co.uk, tel. 020 7246 8357, open Mon-Sat 8:30am-4:30pm, entrance £18, Tube St. Paul's

21 The **Museum of London** recounts the history of London from prehistory until the present. See artwork, drawings and archeological discoveries and learn more about the history of this fascinating city. You'll also get answers to questions such as "Who was Jack the Ripper?" and "What happened during the 1666 great fire of London?"

150 London Wall, www.museumoflondon.org.uk, tel. 020 7001 9844, open daily 10am-6pm, free, Tube Barbican/St. Paul's

22 The **Barbican Centre** is the largest multidisciplinary art center in all of Europe. Various art forms can be found under one roof here, from art and music to dance, theater, and film. For a little break, head to the Barbican Foodhall or the Barbican Lounge.

Silk Street, www.barbican.org.uk, tel. 020 7638 8891, open Mon-Sat 9am-11pm, Sun 11am-11pm, Tube Barbican

23 **St. Bartholomew the Great** is a gorgeous 12th-century church. This charming church has been the set of various films, including *Four Weddings and a Funeral* and *The Other Boleyn Girl*. Be sure to pay attention to the beautiful Tudor Gatehouse as you enter.

West Smithfield, www.greatstbarts.com, tel. 020 7600 0440, open daily, see website for times, entrance £5, Tube Barbican

FOOD & DRINK

7 For culinary inspiration and an overall good time, head to **Maltby Street Market.** This market is made up of two main parts: Ropewalk, the street vendors, and Spa Terminus, the shops under the tracks. Stroll along the various stalls and shops, taste handmade treats, and enjoy the general atmosphere.

Maltby Street, www.maltby.st, open Sat 10am-5pm, Sun 11am-4pm, Tube London Bridge

12 **Arabica Bar & Kitchen** is hidden away inside Borough Market. This restaurant focuses on Levant cuisine and offers a variety of amazingly delicious *mezze*, such as tabbouleh, lahmacun, aubergine (eggplant), kibbeh, and falafel. Come for breakfast, drinks, or anything in between—just be sure to book your table well in advance.

3 Rochester Walk, www.arabicabarandkitchen.com, tel. 020 3011 5151, open Mon-Fri 11:30am-11pm, Sat 9am-11pm, Sun 11:30am-9:30pm, mains from £15, Tube London Bridge

13 For delicious seafood, the incredibly charming **Wright Brothers Borough Market** is the place to go. Make like a local and order a dozen oysters and a pint of Guinness—heavenly!

11 Stoney Street, thewrightbrothers.co.uk/restaurant/borough-market, tel. 020 7403 9554, open Mon-Fri noon-10pm, Sat 11am-11pm, Sun noon-10pm, from £17/half dozen oysters, Tube London Bridge

FACEBOOK THECHEESETRUCK
TWITTER CHEESETRUCKLDN
INSTAGRAM THECHEESETRUCK

LOCAL
BEER HOUSE
OLD
RED COW

⓮ Sunday roast is a traditional British meal that includes meat, potatoes, and roasted vegetables. The restaurant **Roast,** located above the market hall, is the perfect place to enjoy just such a meal. All dishes are made with fresh, local ingredients. This is also a great spot for breakfast.

The Floral Hall, Stoney Street, www.roast-restaurant.com, tel. 020 3006 6111, open Mon-Fri 7am-10:30am, noon-3:30pm & 5:30pm-10:30pm, Sat 8:30am-11:30am, noon-3:30pm & 6pm-8:30pm, Sun 11:30am-6:30pm, from £20, Tube London Bridge

⓯ Monmouth beans are well known in London, and there's no better place to go for a coffee break than **Monmouth Coffee.** It feels just like your living room, only with a view out over the market and bins full of coffee beans. You can also get delicious baguettes, croissants, and cakes here.

2 Park Street, www.monmouthcoffee.co.uk, tel. 020 7232 3010, open Mon-Sat 7:30am-6pm, coffee £2.50, Tube London Bridge

㉔ **The Old Red Cow** is a great place to go for a beer. This charming pub offers a large selection of beers from England, Germany, the United States, and Austria. It also has a variety of ciders. If you get hungry from all that beer, order a hamburger, club sandwich, or shepherd's pie.

71-72 Long Lane, www.theoldredcow.com, tel. 020 7600 6240, open Mon-Thur noon-11pm, Fri-Sat noon-midnight, Sun noon-10:30pm, from £5, Tube Farringdon

㉖ You'll probably have to wait for a table here, because **Polpo Smithfield** doesn't take reservations. Sometimes that wait can be long, but once you've found your way to a table you can choose from a variety of delicious Italian classics, such as spaghetti and meatballs, *linguine vongole*, risotto, and—of course—pizza.

3 Cowcross Street, www.polpo.co.uk, tel. 020 7250 0034, open Mon-Sat 11:30am-11pm, Sun 11:30am-4pm, from £8, Tube Farringdon

㉗ If you're planning on eating at **Hix Oyster & Chop House,** you'd better set aside a few hours for it, because eating here is pure pleasure. The oysters and steak are perfect, and the ambience is simple and stylish. Reservations are recommended.

36-37 Greenhill Rents, Cowcross Street, www.hixoysterandchophouse.co.uk, tel. 020 7017 1930, open Mon-Sat noon-11pm, Sun noon-11pm, from £20, Tube Farringdon

㉘ Hidden down a small street between Clerkenwell Road and Great Sutton Street in a former diamond-cutting factory is **J+A Café.** This is a great spot for delicious breakfast, lunch, or brunch. The menu features healthy, wholesome home cooking from simple recipes that use locally sourced produce. There is always fresh-baked soda bread, a big pot of tea, and a cake on the table. The bar upstairs is nice for drinks.
1-4 Sutton Lane, www.jandacafe.com, tel. 020 7490 2992, open Mon-Fri 8am-5pm, Sat-Sun 9am-5pm, from £5, Tube Barbican

㉙ Breakfast, brunch, lunch, dinner, or drinks—anything is possible at **the Modern Pantry,** which is a café, restaurant, and deli in one. Sit inside, downstairs, upstairs, or outside. This spot is particularly popular on weekends for brunch, so it's best to make reservations then.
47-48 St. John's Square, www.themodernpantry.co.uk, tel. 020 7553 9210, open Mon 8am-11am & noon-9pm, Tue-Fri 8am-11am & noon-10pm, Sat 9am-4pm & 6pm-10pm, Sun 9am-4pm & 5pm-9pm, from £12, Tube Farringdon

㉚ Do you love Asian cuisine? Then come to **Kin,** a restaurant with a minimalist interior where you can order simple yet amazing dishes from all around Asia. Try the Thai curry, Indonesian *nasi goreng*, or the Japanese noodles.
88 Leather Lane, www.kinstreetfood.com, tel. 020 7430 0886, open Mon-Fri noon-3pm & 5:30pm-10:30pm, Sat 5:30pm-10:30pm, from £7, Tube Farringdon/Chancery Lane

㉜ Locals love **Caravan** for breakfast, but this restaurant actually comes highly recommended for any time of day. The menu ranges from delicious French toast to poached eggs, and from salads to sea bass and spicy meatballs. They also roast their own coffee beans.
11-13 Exmouth Market, www.caravanrestaurants.co.uk/exmouth-market.html, tel. 020 7833 8115, open Mon-Fri 8am-10:30pm, Sat 10am-10:30pm, Sun 10am-4pm, from £9, Tube Farringdon

🟤 The mix of Spanish and North African fare at **Moro** is exciting, subtle, and perfect in all its simplicity. Those who are familiar with the Moro cookbook will definitely want to reserve a table here, while those who haven't yet become acquainted with it will certainly want to do so after eating here.

34-36 Exmouth Market, www.moro.co.uk, tel. 020 7833 8336, open Mon-Sat noon-2:30pm & 5:15pm-10:45pm, Sun 12:30pm-3:30pm & 5pm-9:45pm, from £22, Tube Farringdon

🟤 **Sweet** is a bakery with a few tables. Not only do they sell the most delicious baked goods, they also have sandwiches and salads. This is the ideal spot for a quick bite or to quell a hankering for something sweet. But be warned, they are very good at what they do.

64a Exmouth Market, www.sweetdesserts.co.uk, tel. 020 7713 6777, open daily 6:30am-7pm, from £6, Tube Farringdon

SHOPPING

🟤 The cheeses at **Neal's Yard Dairy** come from the British Isles and are served in London's top restaurants. At this cheese shop, you'll also find delicious cheeses to enjoy at home. The staff is determined to help you find just the right cheese to suit your palate, even if that means sampling lots of cheeses in the process.

6 Park Street, Borough Market, www.nealsyarddairy.co.uk, tel. 020 7367 0799, open Mon-Fri 9am-6pm, Sat 8pm-6pm, Tube London Bridge

🟤 Anyone who loves magazines and looking at beautiful photos will surely enjoy spending some time at **Magma Bookshop.** The selection of art, design, architecture, fashion, and music books and magazines is extensive. There are also many great gift items.

117-119 Clerkenwell Road, www.magmabooks.com, tel. 020 7242 9502, open Mon-Sat 10am-7pm, Tube Farringdon/Chancery Lane

㉞ Looking for fun things for your home, kitchen, office, or garden? **Space** is a small shop with a clever collection of unique items and accessories, including ceramics, books, toys, and cards. It's the perfect spot for all your one-of-a-kind gift needs.

25 Exmouth Market, www.ifounditinspace.co.uk, tel. 020 7837 1344, open Mon-Fri 9am-6pm, Sat 10am-6pm, Tube Farringdon

㉟ Marby & Elm is the go-to spot for handmade cards, posters, notebooks, and other printed items. Owner Eleanor Tattersfield makes all of the products herself on the premises of this studio-cum-shop with an old-fashioned letterpress.

53 Exmouth Market, www.marbyandelm.com, tel. 079 0341 9661, open Mon-Fri 10am-6pm, Sat 11am-5pm, Sun noon-5pm, Tube Farringdon

MORE TO EXPLORE

① Dating back to the 14th century, **Leadenhall Market** is one of London's oldest covered markets. The beautiful, ornate roof was designed by Sir Horace Jones in 1881 and is certainly worth noticing. Come here for a variety of shops, cafés, and restaurants, including Barbour, The Good Yard, and The Lamb Tavern. The market also serves as a popular location for film shoots, and can be seen in movies including *Harry Potter and the Sorcerer's Stone*.

Gracechurch Street, www.leadenhallmarket.co.uk, tel. 020 7332 1523, open Mon-Fri, hours vary, Tube Bank/Monument

② London has its fair share of skyscrapers and the "Walkie Talkie" is one of the latest additions. This 37-story office building stands 525 feet tall and features the **Sky Garden** at its very top: a wide-open space with landscaped gardens full of exotic plants. The view out over the city from here is phenomenal. The rooftop also houses several restaurants—Sky Pod Bar, Darwin Brasserie, and Fenchurch Seafood Bar & Grill—that are open morning, noon, and night. Just be sure to book in advance.

20 Fenchurch Street, skygarden.london, tel. 020 7337 2344, open Mon-Fri 10am-6pm, Sat-Sun 11am-9pm, free, Tube Monument

④ The marina **St. Katharine Docks** is directly next to the City. You'll see business men and women in perfectly tailored suits pop over here for a quick lunch. The marina is a little slice of calm next to the bustling area around Tower Bridge and is perhaps one of the best-kept secrets in London.
50 St. Katharine's Way, www.skdocks.co.uk, tel. 020 7264 5312, Tube Tower Hill

⑥ **Butler's Wharf** is the collective name of the complex of renovated warehouses, restaurants, stores, and apartment buildings on the south side of the Thames. It's nice to walk around here and sit outside at one of the restaurants where there is an amazing view of Tower Bridge.
Shad Thames, Tube Tower Hill/London Bridge

🔆 **Borough Market** is one of London's biggest and oldest markets. From Wednesday to Saturday, vendors and suppliers come here from around the country to sell some of the most delicious items—fruits and vegetables, fish on ice, freshly made bread, chocolate, meat, jam, and olives, and so much more.
Borough Market, www.boroughmarket.org.uk, tel. 020 7407 1002, open Mon-Thur 10am-5pm, Fri 10am-6pm, Sat 8am-5pm, Tube London Bridge

⑰ Shakespeare's **Globe Theatre** is a reconstruction of the original theater where many of Shakespeare's best-known plays were first performed. There are performances here from April to October. It is just as it would have been during Shakespeare's time: standing in the open air or sitting on wooden benches. The rest of the year, it is still an interesting spot to visit and tours run year-round.
21 New Globe Walk, Bankside, www.shakespearesglobe.com, tel. 020 7401 9919, open daily, see website for times, performances start at £17 (standing tickets £5), Tube Southwark/St. Paul's

㉕ For the past 800 years, meat has been bought and sold at **Smithfield Market.** The beautiful Victorian building dates from 1867. If you want to see the market in full swing, you'd better get here early—preferably before 7am.
Charterhouse Street, www.smithfieldmarket.com, tel. 020 7332 3092, open Mon-Fri 2am-noon, Tube Farringdon/Barbican

SHOREDITCH

ABOUT THE WALK

This route takes you to the artistic part of the city. You'll go past art galleries, vintage boutiques, and creative markets. The streets around Shoreditch are interesting, and for those wanting to explore more nice spots, you can also deviate from the route and head further through East London. Many places on this route also make this great for nightlife.

THE NEIGHBORHOODS

Shoreditch is in the East End. Traditionally this was the working-class part of the city. However, with the arrival of artists and the creative sector in the late 1980s, Shoreditch has transformed into one of the hippest neighborhoods in London. Here, there are more artists per square mile than in any other part of Europe. Controversial artwork, the newest hypes, and the latest trends all have their beginnings in Shoreditch. Although rent has continued to inch upward, the artsy vibe has remained, and you see this in all of the street art here, including the graffiti-clad walls and the industrial warehouses that are home to creative companies. Large chains are slowly taking over the neighborhood, pushing the true trendsetters farther and farther east.

Shoreditch is not only popular for its creative vibe, but also for its nightlife. Clubs, pubs, restaurants, markets, and coffee shops—it's got it all. The neighborhood is also home to Asian and other international communities that contribute to making this artistic melting pot such a fascinating place. There are famous streets such as **Brick Lane,** which is also known as Banglatown. Londoners come here for the only true national dish: curry!

North of Shoreditch, the neighborhood of **Hoxton** saw a similar trajectory of working-class neighborhood transformed by an influx of artists and students. Where Old Street meets Hoxton Street is the epicenter of the bars, restaurants, and clubs that make for a fun night out, but head farther north for the Hoxton Hall performance venue or for **Hoxton Street Monster Supplies,** a shop dedicated to all things that go bump in the night.

SHORT ON TIME? HERE ARE THE HIGHLIGHTS:

① WHITECHAPEL GALLERY + ② BRICK LANE + ④ SUNDAY UPMARKET + ⑭ COLUMBIA ROAD + ㉒ BOXPARK SHOREDITCH

TIPS

// This is a young, hip, and creative neighborhood // Good for a Sunday walk, thanks to all the markets // A great spot to experience London nightlife

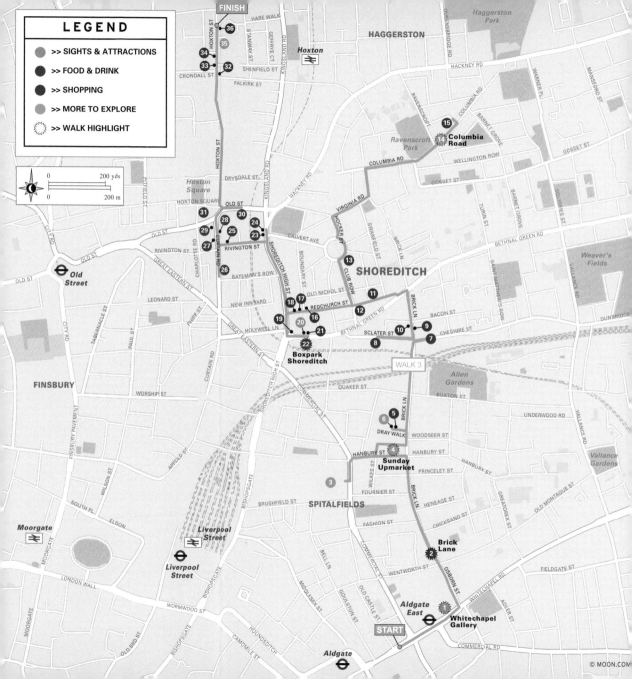

LEGEND

- ● >> SIGHTS & ATTRACTIONS
- ● >> FOOD & DRINK
- ● >> SHOPPING
- ● >> MORE TO EXPLORE
- ☼ >> WALK HIGHLIGHT

0   200 yds
0   200 m

FINISH

HAGGERSTON

Hoxton

HAGGERSTON PARK

QUEENSBRIDGE RD

HARE WALK

HACKNEY RD

Columbia
Road

15
14

Ravenscroft
Park

COLUMBIA RD

WELLINGTON ROW

GOSSET ST

VIRGINIA RD

SHOREDITCH

13

CALVERT AVE

11

REDCHURCH ST

12

BETHNAL GREEN RD

BRICK LN

SCLATER ST

8   10   9
7

WALK 3

Allen
Gardens

BUXTON ST

UNDERWOOD RD

Vallance
Gardens

DRAY WALK

6   5

WOODSEER ST

HANBURY ST

Sunday
Upmarket

PRINCELET ST

3

FOURNIER ST

SPITALFIELDS

FASHION ST

HENEAGE ST

CHICKSAND ST

Brick
Lane

2

BRICK LN

OSBORN ST

OLD MONTAGUE ST

Moorgate

Liverpool
Street

Liverpool
Street

BISHOPSGATE

FINSBURY

Old
Street

Old Street

OLD ST

RIVINGTON ST

31
29   28   30   24
27   25   23
26

Hoxton
Square

HOXTON SQUARE

OLD ST

DRYSDALE ST

HOXTON ST

36
35
34
33   32

CRONDALL ST

FALKIRK ST

SHENFIELD ST

KINGSLAND RD

HACKNEY RD

Bateman's Row

NEW INN YARD

18   17
16
19   20   21
22

Boxpark
Shoreditch

HOLYWELL LN

GREAT EASTERN ST

CURTAIN RD

WORSHIP ST

SHOREDITCH HIGH ST

COMMERCIAL ST

QUAKER ST

BRUSHFIELD ST

HANBURY ST

WILKES ST

WENTWORTH ST

Aldgate
East

1

Whitechapel
Gallery

WHITECHAPEL RD

COMMERCIAL RD

START

Aldgate

© MOON.COM

WALK 3 DESCRIPTION (approx. 4.5 mi/7 km)

A stone's throw from Aldgate East station you'll find the Whitechapel Gallery ①. After the gallery turn left on Osborn Street and continue straight onto Brick Lane ②. Turn left on Hanbury Street, then left again on Commercial Street to Spitalfields Market ③. Head back to Hanbury Street to Sunday Upmarket ④. Exit the market on Brick Lane and go left, then turn left again down the alley Dray Walk to check out some music ⑤ ⑥. Back at Brick Lane continue to the left. A few blocks down, turn right to go shopping on Cheshire Street ⑦ or left on Sclater Street for Lik & Neon ⑧. Then continue back on Brick Lane ⑨ ⑩ and turn left to get to Redchurch Street, where there's a nice shop that sells items for the kitchen, home and garden ⑪. Head to Barber and Parlour ⑫ for breakfast, lunch, or coffee. Or turn right and take Club Row to Arnold Circus and enjoy a meal in a former school building ⑬. On the other side of the roundabout, head down Hocker Street, then turn right on Virginia Road, and right again on Columbia Road to reach the flower market ⑭ ⑮. Not up for the market? Then head back to Redchurch Street for more great places to eat and shop ⑯ ⑰ ⑱. To the left, at the corner of Shoreditch High Street and Bethnal Green Road, you'll find Pizza East ⑲, Hales Gallery ⑳ and Lyle's ㉑, and across the street is the pop-up mall Boxpark Shoreditch ㉒. From there, walk back up Shoreditch High Street for more retail fun ㉓ ㉔. Then walk back a bit and turn right on Rivington Street to sip some cocktails ㉕. Head left on Curtain Road, which will take you to the Hoxton Pony ㉖, then head back in the direction you came from to check out two nice shops and enjoy some good old BBQ and blues ㉗ ㉘ ㉙. At the end of Curtain Road, turn right on Old Street to get to The Clove Club ㉚ or cross over to Rufus Street for all-day breakfast ㉛. Then go north on Hoxton Street (on the right if coming from The Clove Club, on the left if coming from The Breakfast Club) for some restaurants, a shop, and a concert hall ㉜ ㉝ ㉞ ㉟ ㊱.

SIGHTS & ATTRACTIONS

1 For innovative, contemporary art exhibitions, there is no better place to go in London than **Whitechapel Gallery.** Exhibitions change regularly, and there are often also interesting readings here. It may not be as well known as Tate Modern, but it is certainly just as nice.

77-82 Whitechapel High Street, www.whitechapelgallery.org, tel. 020 7522 7888, open Tue-Wed & Fri-Sun 11am-6pm, Thur 11am-9pm, free, Tube Aldgate East

20 When it comes to modern and contemporary art, **Hales Gallery** is the place to be. Founders Paul Hedge and Paul Maslin opened their first space in Deptford more than two decades ago. They have been in Shoreditch since 2004 and now also have a space in New York. Exhibitions include works by up-and-coming artists and by internationally established names such as Carolee Schneemann, Michael Smith, and Hew Locke.

7 Bethnal Green Road, www.halesgallery.com, tel. 020 7033 1938, open Wed-Sat 11am-6pm, Overground Shoreditch High Street

FOOD & DRINK

2 There is such a large Bangladeshi community in this neighborhood that under the English language street sign for **Brick Lane** there's also one in Bengali. Many of the countless restaurants here originally served as homes away from home for the migrant workers who had left their families behind. Today people from all over London flock to Banglatown, as the area is known, for Britain's only true national dish: chicken tikka masala. There are plenty of curry houses to choose from on Brick Lane, and you'll always find a place for a delicious meal.

Brick Lane, www.visitbricklane.org, open daily, Tube Aldgate East/Liverpool Street

9 As the name suggests, **Cereal Killer Café** specializes in cereal. There are more than one hundred kinds on offer here, from peanut butter-covered oatmeal to cornflakes topped with marshmallows or banana. The walls of this colorful hipster café are covered in, you guessed it, cereal boxes that are sourced from all over the world. They include everything from the familiar Kellogg's boxes to hard-to-find collector's items.

192a Brick Lane, www.cerealkillercafe.co.uk, tel. 020 3601 9100, open daily 8am-10pm, cereal £6, Overground Shoreditch High Street

⑩ Chocolate lovers might want to keep walking because it is difficult to resist all the tempting chocolate at **Dark Sugars.** Chocolate truffles are displayed here in large wooden bowls alongside an assortment of chocolate bonbons—all with amazing flavor combinations. Try chocolate flavors such as ginger and honey, cardamom, cognac, or coffee and walnut.

141 Brick Lane, www.darksugars.co.uk, tel. 074 2947 2606, open daily 10am-10pm, 7 truffles £8, Overground Shoreditch High Street

⑫ **Barber & Parlour** is a barber shop, nail studio, and café all in one. Head to the café for a coffee, breakfast, brunch, or a glass of wine. While you're there, treat yourself to a haircut, manicure, or beard trim. They do it all. There's also a movie theater in the building, in case you're up for a flick after all that pampering.

64-66 Redchurch Street, www.barberandparlour.com, tel. 020 3376 1777, open daily 9am-10pm, breakfast £8, Overground Shoreditch High Street

⑬ Shh, **Rochelle Canteen** is the "in" crowd's little secret, so mum's the word. This restaurant is open only during the week, and it is difficult to find. Ring the bell that says "canteen" at the place where the boys' entrance to this old school was, and a culinary adventure awaits you. The restaurant, located in the old bike shed, serves up a daily menu of British fare—with a twist, *of course.*

Rochelle School, Arnold Circus, www.arnoldandhenderson.com/rochelle-canteen, tel. 020 7729 5667, open Sun-Wed 9am-11am & noon-3pm, Thur-Sat 9am-11am & noon-3pm & 6pm-9pm, from £10, Tube Shoreditch High Street/Old Street

⑮ Get delicious sandwiches, cakes, and pastries at the **Lily Vanilli Bakery,** and then bring them to one of the wooden tables inside or in the charming courtyard to enjoy. This is definitely the place to come if you're in the mood for a cup of tea and something yummy.

6 The Courtyard, Ezra Street, www.lilyvanilli.com, open Sun 8:30am-4.30pm, Overground Hoxton

16 In the basement of the fantastic Boundary Hotel sits the eponymous restaurant, and upstairs is a great rooftop bar. However, the biggest attraction here is undoubtedly the café and bakery **Albion.** Come here for an early breakfast, a late dinner, and a moment in between. The menu is full of British favorites, and the food is always delicious.
2-4 Boundary Street, www.boundary.london/albion, tel. 020 7729 1051, open daily 8am-11pm, from £10, Overground Shoreditch High Street

18 Peruvian cuisine has long been a hit in London. **Andina** is a colorful restaurant where you can get classic Peruvian dishes such as ceviche—raw fish marinated in tiger's milk. During the day, come here for breakfast or lunch with fresh-pressed Peruvian juice, and at night enjoy a variety of types of ceviche and cocktails to go with it.
1 Redchurch Street, www.andinalondon.com/shoreditch, tel. 020 7920 6499, open Mon-Fri 8am-11pm, Sat-Sun 10am-11pm, from £9, Overground Shoreditch High Street

19 Where you see the giant letters "T-E-A" up on the roof you'll find **Pizza East.** The big industrial space makes it less than ideal for an intimate dinner, but it is perfect for a fun night out with friends. The pizzas and antipasti here are out of this world.
56 Shoreditch High Street, www.pizzaeast.com, tel. 020 7729 1888, open Mon-Wed noon-midnight, Thur noon-1am, Fri noon-2am, Sat 10am-2am, Sun 10am-midnight, from £12, Tube Shoreditch High Street/Old Street

21 For an elaborate sit-down lunch or a special dinner, head to **Lyle's.** The restaurant, with its light and airy minimalist décor, offers a modern take on classic British fare. In the evenings, Chef James Lowe serves up a four-course set menu, whereas for lunch you can choose from a variety of smaller dishes à la carte.
Tea Building, 56 Shoreditch High Street, www.lyleslondon.com, tel. 020 3011 5911, open Mon-Fri 8am-11pm, Sat noon-11pm, mains from £59, Overground Shoreditch High Street

㉕ Callooh Callay Bar is a cocktail bar that oozes character, with a stand-out interior and feel-good vibe. The service is friendly, and the cocktails are amazing. On the menu you'll find all the classics as well as an assortment of original mixed drinks, perhaps made with London gin, various liqueurs, or vodka. There's also a selection of nibbles to choose from.

65 Rivington Street, www.calloohcallaybar.com, tel. 020 7739 4781, open daily 6pm-1am, cocktails starting at £10, Tube Old Street

㉖ For delicious cocktails and a swinging evening, **the Hoxton Pony** is the perfect spot. The "Tea Party," which includes cocktails from teapots and plates of delicious snacks, is particularly fun. Reservations are a good idea (and bring along your confirmation number).

104-108 Curtain Road, www.thehoxtonpony.com, tel. 020 3409 3636, open Fri-Sat 7pm-2am, cocktails from £8, Tube Shoreditch High Street/Old Street

㉘ For an evening of blues and rock 'n' roll, head to **The Blues Kitchen.** Enjoy some ribs, pulled pork, or a good burger and refreshing libations while you take in the live music. Blues and soul performances are recurring events here. Those who prefer a more exclusive night out can rent the Airstream caravan and host their own private party.

134-146 Curtain Road, www.theblueskitchen.com/shoreditch, tel. 020 7729 7216, open Sun 11am-10:30pm, Mon-Wed noon-midnight, Thur noon-1am, Fri noon-2:30am, Sat 11am-3am, meals £14, Overground Shoreditch High Street

㉚ When you have something really important to celebrate, head to **The Clove Club.** It has everything you would expect from a Michelin-starred restaurant: exquisite food, beautiful presentation, a fabulous interior, and top-notch service. The six-course menu comes highly recommended. Of course, you need an advance reservation here.

Shoreditch Town Hall, 380 Old Street, www.thecloveclub.com, tel. 020 7729 6496, open Mon 6pm-10:30pm, Tue-Sat noon-1:45pm & 6pm-10:30pm, six-course menu £95, Tube Old Street

㉛ The Breakfast Club is a great place for breakfast, which is served here all day long. The menu includes dishes such as scrambled eggs with salmon, pancakes with syrup, and a variety of burritos, wraps, and sandwiches. The restaurant has a nice mix of old tables and chairs, a lost parasol, and a really laid-back ambience.

2-4 Rufus Street, www.thebreakfastclubcafes.com, tel. 020 7729 5252, open Mon-Wed 8am-11pm, Thur-Sat 8am-midnight, Sun 8am-10pm, from £8, Tube Shoreditch High Street/Old Street

㉜ Whether you're in the mood for a full breakfast or just a cup of coffee and toast, **The Bach** (pronounced "batch") is the place to be for "brekkie" and brunch. The café's name comes from the New Zealand word for beach house—an important part of New Zealand culture and, like this restaurant, the perfect spot to relax and unwind.

98 Hoxton Street, www.wearethebach.com, tel. 020 7683 1591, open Mon-Fri 7:30am-5pm, Sat-Sun 8am-5pm, brunch £8, Overground Hoxton

㉝ Delicious, sustainable food and great drinks are what you can expect to find at **Cub.** Owner Ryan "Mr. Lyan" Chetiyawardana has plenty of awards to his name, and after sampling the food here, it's obvious why. The charming, retro color scheme and wooden furniture make you feel right at home. Reservations are recommended because the restaurant is open only four nights a week.

153 Hoxton Street, www.lyancub.com, tel. 020 3693 3202, open Wed-Sat 6pm-midnight, set menu £67, Overground Hoxton

㊱ If you're in the mood for some traditional pie and mash, you've come to the right place. **F. Cooke** has been serving up this typical East London fare since 1862. The signature dish consists of savory meat pie with mashed potatoes and a parsley sauce referred to as "liquor." You can also order the eels and mash version.

150 Hoxton Street, tel. 020 7729 7718, open Mon-Thur 10am-7pm, Fri-Sat 9:30am-8pm, pie & mash £4.75, Overground Hoxton

SHOPPING

⑤ Rough Trade East is a music store, coffee shop, stage, and Internet café in one. Music aficionados will be able to spend hours here. If you're lucky, your favorite band might just be performing as you browse around.

The Old Truman Brewery, 91 Brick Lane, www.roughtrade.com, tel. 020 7392 7788, open Mon-Thur 9am-9pm, Fri 9am-8pm, Sat 10am-8pm, Sun 11am-7pm, Tube Liverpool Street

⑦ Cheshire Street is a side street of Brick Lane and has some of the most original stores, such as House of Vintage and Beyond Retro, which have fantastic vintage clothes, and Mar Mar Co, which has a variety of good-looking design items. Discover beautiful, exclusive jewelry at Comfort Station, and don't forget Duke of Uke, London's only true ukulele and banjo shop.

Cheshire Street, open daily, Tube Shoreditch High Street/Old Street

8 Behind **Lik & Neon's** bright neon orange storefront you'll find a sleek interior. This tiny shop has T-shirts, CDs, newspapers, accessories, and other random items, all of which are equally fun and unique.
106 Sclater Street, likneon.bigcartel.com, open Mon noon-7pm, Tue-Sat 11am-7pm, Sun 11am-6:30pm, Tube Shoreditch High Street/Old Street

11 Looking for nice things for your home, garden, or kitchen? At **Labour and Wait** you'll find a mix of timeless home accessories and stylish gift ideas. The odds are you won't be able to leave here empty-handed.
85 Redchurch Street, www.labourandwait.co.uk, tel. 020 7729 6253, open Tue-Fri 11am-6:30pm, Sat-Sun 11am-6pm, Overground Shoreditch High Street

17 The brand **Sunspel** has been around for more than 150 years and has several stores across London. Here you'll find timeless, comfortable polo shirts, sweaters, and underwear for men.
7 Redchurch Street, www.sunspel.com, tel. 020 7739 9729, open Mon-Sat 11am-7pm, Sun noon-5pm, Overground Shoreditch High Street

22 **Boxpark Shoreditch** is the world's first pop-up shopping center. Stacked containers have been magically transformed into stores, cafés, and galleries where you'll find fashion and lifestyle brands such as Vagabond, Filling Pieces, and Urbanears. It's a completely new shopping experience.
2-4 Bethnal Green Road, www.boxpark.co.uk, open shops open Mon-Wed & Fri-Sat 11am-7pm, Thur 11am-8pm, Sun noon-6pm, cafés and galleries open Mon-Sat 8am-11pm, Sun 10am-10pm, Tube Shoreditch High Street

23 **Aida** is a concept store that specializes in men's and women's clothing and accessories with a vintage twist, from brands including Bruuns Bazaar, Olivia Burton, Selected Femme, Paco Milan, and Mads Norgaard. When you're finished shopping, stop for a tasty lunch or cup of coffee at the small café in the front of the store.

133 Shoreditch High Street, www.aidashoreditch.co.uk, tel. 020 7739 2811, open
Sun noon-6pm, Mon-Sat 10:30am-7pm, Overground Shoreditch High Street

24 The couple Javvy M Royle and Frieda Gormley founded **House of Hackney**
in 2010. It is a small designer department store that sells only English designs,
including furniture, home accessories, clothing, textiles, wallpaper, and
stationery—all covered in the most gorgeous prints.
131 Shoreditch High Street, www.houseofhackney.com, tel. 020 7739 3901, open
Mon-Sat 10am-7pm, Sun 11am-5pm, Overground Shoreditch High Street

27 If you love home furnishings, there will be plenty of things at **SCP** you'll
want to put on your wish list. Items by contemporary British designers, such as
Terence Woodgate, Matthew Hilton, and Tom Dixon are showcased here side by
side with classic designs by Verner Panton and Eileen Gray.
135-139 Curtain Road, www.scp.co.uk, tel. 020 7739 1869, open Mon-Sat 9:30am-
6pm, Sun 11am-5pm, Tube Shoreditch High Street/Old Street

29 With its extensive collections of women's, men's, and children's wear as well
as shoes, jewelry, accessories, cosmetics, and home furnishings, you could
easily spend hours browsing **The Goodhood Store.** You'll find more than 200
brands here, some well known and others yet to be discovered, including
Opening Ceremony, Converse, Nanushka, Junya Watanabe, and Paul Smith.
There really is something for everyone here.
151 Curtain Road, www.goodhoodstore.com, tel. 020 7729 3600, open Sun noon-6pm,
Mon-Fri 10:30am-6:30pm, Sat 10:30am-7pm, Overground Shoreditch High Street

34 **Hoxton Street Monster Supplies** is the only store in London, and perhaps
even in the world, that caters to monsters and other nightmarish creatures. For
centuries the store has welcomed werewolves, vampires, and other fantastic
beings as its clientele. Products include food, notebooks, and T-shirts, often
with funny and frightening texts. The store's proceeds go to the Ministry of
Stories, a charity that helps foster the writing skills of children in East London.
159 Hoxton Street, www.monstersupplies.org, tel. 020 7729 4159, open Thur-Fri
1pm-5pm, Sat 11am-5pm, Overground Hoxton

MORE TO EXPLORE

3 In recent years **Spitalfields Market** has been modernized, and an increasing number of big chains have moved in, somewhat affecting the market. Nonetheless stores such as Belstaff and Collectif and restaurants such as Taberna do Mercado and Blixen, which have great lunches, still make this a great place to come and shop—especially on Thurdays or Fridays, when there are stalls with antiques and vintage items, and clothes and art, respectively. If you go on Sunday, all of the stalls will be open, but you'll also have to contend with the crowds.

16 Horner Square, www.oldspitalfieldsmarket.com, open Sun 10am-5pm, Mon-Fri 10am-8pm, Sat 10am-6pm, Tube Liverpool Street

4 **Sunday Upmarket,** in the old Truman Brewery, is the perfect spot to come to buy unique, handmade products directly from the designer or maker. More than 140 vendors sell clothes, art, and delicious baked goods here. The vibe is something like Spitalfields of yesteryear.

The Old Truman Brewery, 91 Brick Lane, www.sundayupmarket.co.uk, tel. 020 7770 6028, open Sun 10am-5pm, Tube Aldgate East/Liverpool Street

⑥ The Big Chill is an annual festival and record label that will take you back in time. The bar, the **Big Chill Bar,** ensures you can enjoy the Big Chill vibe every day. Generally speaking, the music is fantastic.

Dray Walk, the Old Truman Brewery, wearebigchill.com, tel. 020 7392 9180, open Sun-Thur noon-midnight, Fri-Sat noon-1am, glass of wine £8, Tube Liverpool Street

⑭ Every Sunday, **Columbia Road** is in full bloom with the Columbia Road Market. This flower market attracts Londoners with green fingers, but it's the shops and cafés that make it really fun. Head to Jones Dairy for yummy bagels or to Treacle for delicious cupcakes. Angela Flanders has unique perfumes, Supernice sells hip wall stickers, and Ryantown is the shop of paper artist Rob Ryan—and that's just for starters.

Columbia Road, www.columbiaroad.info, open market Sun 8am-3pm, Tube Old Street

㉟ **Hoxton Hall** has been around since 1863 and is a great place to go for a concert, a play, or another performance showcasing England's creative talent. Swing dance and stand-up comedy events are also held here. Most performances are small, independent, and highly original productions, which means an evening here is guaranteed to be one you'll remember.

130 Hoxton Street, www.hoxtonhall.co.uk, tel. 020 7684 0060, Overground Hoxton

KING'S CROSS & ANGEL

ABOUT THE WALK

This walk will take you through two neighborhoods: King's Cross and Angel. King's Cross is one of the rapidly changing areas of London. New hotspots are popping up here left and right. Angel is not the ideal place to start if you've never been to London before—the focus here is mainly on eating, drinking, and shopping.

THE NEIGHBORHOODS

In the northern part of central London, you'll find two increasingly popular neighborhoods: King's Cross and Angel.

King's Cross in particular is changing very rapidly. Not too long ago this neighborhood was plagued by prostitution and crime, but since the 1990s it has undergone a significant transformation. With the arrival of the Eurostar in 2007 and significant renovations to King's Cross/St. Pancras International and surrounding dilapidated buildings, King's Cross has become a completely different place.

Granary Square is a great example of all this development. This square is surrounded by renovated warehouses that are now home to trendy restaurants and the famous fashion school Central Saint Martins. Around Granary Square, an entirely new neighborhood has gone up. Once all of the construction is complete, King's Cross will have some twenty new streets, 2,000 new homes, and close to 11,000 square feet (1,000 square meters) of new retail, office, and living space. This is definitely a neighborhood to keep an eye on.

About a ten-minute walk to the east you'll find **Islington,** and at its center the charming **Angel.** This is a bustling neighborhood known for its streets Upper

Street and Essex Road. You won't find any big museums or tourist attractions here, but you will find an enormous selection of stores, pubs, theaters, and restaurants. In addition, this neighborhood is really close to the financial center known as "The City" and the creative neighborhood of Clerkenwell. It is also a popular, diverse residential neighborhood where you'll find a mix of students, young families, and career-focused couples.

SHORT ON TIME? HERE ARE THE HIGHLIGHTS:
⑩ GRANARY SQUARE + ⑬ KINGS PLACE + ⑳ SADLER'S WELLS + ㉑ CAMDEN PASSAGE + ㉗ OTTOLENGHI

TIPS
// Good route if you've been to London before
// The many restaurants and bars make this an ideal evening destination
// Recommended for theater lovers

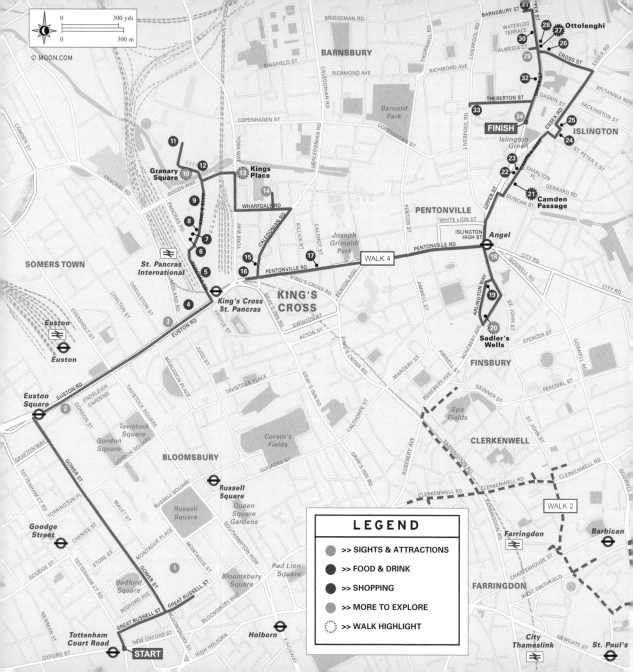

WALK 4 DESCRIPTION (approx. 6 mi/10 km)

From the Tottenham Court Road Tube station take Tottenham Court Road and Great Russell Street directly to the British Museum ❶. Then walk back a bit and turn right on Bloomsbury Street, which turns into Gower Street. At the end of the street turn right on Euston Road to visit the Wellcome Collection ❷ and, further on, the British Library ❸. Keep going for a meal at the Booking Office ❹ in the St. Pancras Renaissance London Hotel. Or walk on and turn left on Pancras Road to eat at Plum + Spilt Milk ❺ or one of several other good restaurants ❻ ❼ ❽. Turn right on King's Boulevard for lunch at Maple & King's ❾, then continue on to Granary Square ❿. This is an excellent place for dinner and shopping ⓫ ⓬. Walk back over the bridge and turn left on Goods Way for music and theater ⓭. From York Way, turn left on Wharfdale Road and left again to visit the London Canal Museum ⓮. Walk back and continue on Wharfdale Road, then turn right on Caledonian Road to Drink, Shop & Do ⓯. Continue straight and turn right on Pentonville Road, then right again on Regent Quarter for tapas ⓰. Otherwise, turn left on Pentonville Road to Mildreds ⓱ and in the direction of Angel, about a 15-minute walk. From King's Cross station you can also get the bus or the tube—if you take the Northern Line underground, Angel is the next stop. If you're walking, turn right at the end of Pentonville Road on St. John Street to the Old Red Lion Theatre ⓲. Continue on St. John Street, turn right on Chadwell Street, then immediately left on Arlington Way for stationery at Present & Correct ⓳ and the Sadler's Wells dance theater ⓴. Walk around and take Rosebery Avenue back to St. John Street and continue straight onto Islington High Street. Turn right on Duncan Street and immediately left toward Camden Passage for shopping ㉑ ㉒ and a bite to eat ㉓. Continue straight past Islington Green to Essex Road. To the right is Colebrooke Row ㉔ ㉕. Continue on Essex Road and turn left on Cross Street for some shopping ㉖. This will take you to Upper Street, where there are great places to eat and shop ㉗ ㉘, take in a show at the theater ㉙, and shop some more ㉚ ㉛ ㉜. For a nice pub, take Theberton Street and make an immediate left on Liverpool Road ㉝. Or you can end the evening with a movie at Screen on the Green ㉞.

SIGHTS & ATTRACTIONS

1 With more than 5 million visitors annually, the **British Museum** is hands down London's most visited attraction—and not for nothing. The collection is second to none. Here you'll find Egyptian and Asian collections, as well as an enormous collection of Greek and Roman art among other things.
Great Russell Street, www.britishmuseum.org, tel. 020 7323 8000, open Sat-Thur 10am-5:30pm, Fri 10am-8:30pm, free, Tube Tottenham Court Road/Holborn

2 At the **Wellcome Collection,** science, medicine, art, and life are brought together in a unique way in a series of exhibitions. The museum is named after Sir Henry Wellcome, a famous pharmacist, philanthropist, and collector. Don't forget to visit the Wellcome Café for a cup of coffee and a yummy bite to eat.
183 Euston Road, www.wellcomecollection.org, tel. 020 7611 2222, open Tue-Wed & Fri-Sat 10am-6pm, Thur 10am-10pm, free, Tube Euston Square/Euston

3 With more than 150 million books, magazines, and documents in its collection, the **British Library** is one of the largest libraries in the world. Only members are allowed in the reading room, but there are also exhibitions, events, and tours that allow you see and enjoy this stately building. Here you'll also find a store, café, and restaurant.
96 Euston Road, www.bl.uk, tel. 084 3208 1144, open Mon-Thur 9:30am-8pm, Fri 9:30am-6pm, Sat 9:30am-5pm, Sun 11am-5pm, Tube King's Cross/St. Pancras

14 The **London Canal Museum** is located in a former ice house. This small museum is dedicated entirely to London's canals. It's particularly fun to take a boat trip—and some tour boats stop here. Tours will take you over Regent's Canal and past Little Venice, London Zoo, and Camden Town.
12-13 New Wharf Road, www.canalmuseum.org.uk, tel. 020 7713 0836, open Tue-Sun 10am-4:30pm, entrance £5, Tube King's Cross

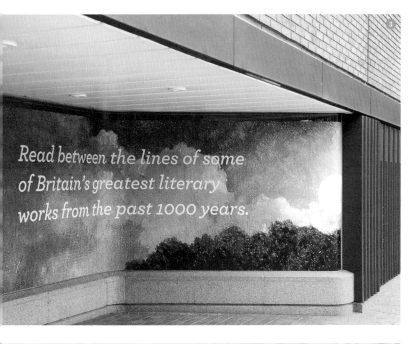

Read between the lines of some of Britain's greatest literary works from the past 1000 years.

FOOD & DRINK

❹ Around 1860, train tickets were sold in the **Booking Office.** Today this historical space serves as the bar and restaurant in the St. Pancras Renaissance Hotel. The space has high brick walls, a 95-foot-long (29-meter-long) bar, and elements that would not be out of place in a cathedral, and you can come here to enjoy a delicious breakfast, lunch, dinner, or a nice drink.

Euston Road, www.stpancraslondon.com, tel. 020 7841 3566, open Mon-Wed 6:30am-midnight, Thur-Sat 6:30am-1am, Sun 7am-midnight, from £18, Tube King's Cross/St. Pancras

❺ In the newly renovated Great Northern Hotel you'll find **Plum + Spilt Milk,** an elegant restaurant where you can start the day off with a nice breakfast or where you can come in the evening for drinks that turn into a late dinner. The interior is stylish with designer lighting and dark furniture, and the food is a modern take on British fare.

Great Northern Hotel, Pancras Road, www.plumandspiltmilk.com, tel. 020 3388 0818, open Mon-Fri 7am-11pm, Sat 8am-11pm, Sun 8am-10pm, from £20, Tube King's Cross

❻ In a former German gymnasium, built in 1865, sits the eponymously named restaurant **German Gymnasium.** In 1866 the venue hosted events from London's first Olympic Games, and today it is home to a stylish restaurant with a grand café and bar where you can eat and drink to your heart's content from early morning until late at night. The menu includes European cuisine with a German twist from Chef Bjoern Wassmuth.

1 King's Boulevard, www.germangymnasium.com, tel. 020 7287 8000, open Sun 10am-10pm, Mon-Wed 8am-midnight, Thur-Fri 8am-1am, Sat 10am-1am, from £10, Tube King's Cross

❼ **Granger & Co.** is a popular restaurant run by Australian chef Bill Granger. Come here any time of day from early in the morning to late at night for a delicious, healthy meal. The menu features tempting dishes such as fresh fruit with Greek yogurt and açaí bowls for breakfast, tuna and avocado lunchtime salads, and shrimp burgers for dinner. They don't take reservations, so bear in mind that you might need to wait for a table.

Stanley Building, 7 Pancras Square, www.grangerandco.com, tel. 020 3058 2567, open Sun 8am-10:30pm, Mon-Sat 7am-11pm, mains from £16, Tube King's Cross

❽ For wine lovers, a visit to **Vinoteca** is mandatory. Besides great wine, you can also enjoy delicious food in the restaurant. The shop has more than 200 wines available for purchase. With a selection ranging from affordable to pricier wines from all around the world, there's plenty to choose from.

3 King's Boulevard, www.vinoteca.co.uk, tel. 020 3793 7210, open Sun 10am-10pm, Mon-Fri 7:30am-11pm, Sat 10am-11pm, bottle of wine starting at £8.50, Tube King's Cross

❾ At **Maple & King's** you can enjoy a healthy breakfast, brunch, or lunch all day long. Order any of the fresh juices, smoothies, or a good cup of coffee and a bowl of porridge, avocado toast, or a fresh salad made with local ingredients. Eat in or get your meal to go.

Unit 1, 3 Pancras Square, www.mymapleandco.com, tel. 020 3479 1988, open Mon-Tue & Fri 8am-7pm, Wed-Thur 8am-8pm, lunch £7, Tube King's Cross

⓬ **The Lighterman**—a three-tiered restaurant, bar, and pub—is one of Granary Square's latest additions. In the summer the terrace is a lovely place to sit outside, and in the winter you can enjoy a wonderful view of the canal and Granary Square from indoors. The menu offers classic British fare with European influences, and there is also a good selection of beer, wine, and cocktails.

3 Granary Square, www.thelighterman.co.uk, tel. 020 3846 3400, open Sun 9am-10:30pm, Mon-Thur 8am-11:30pm, Fri 8am-midnight, Sat 9am-midnight, mains from £18, Tube King's Cross

⓯ **Drink, Shop & Do** is a design store, café, and overall great place to go. Come here for an afternoon of hanging out, afternoon tea, or an evening of dancing and cocktails. The venue has a nostalgic feel, thanks to the retro

furniture and the cheerful use of colors. Everything here is for sale, from the artwork on the walls to the dishes, homemade cakes, and vintage furniture.
9 Caledonian Road, www.drinkshopdo.co.uk, tel. 020 7278 4335, open Mon-Wed 10am-midnight, Thur 10am-1am, Fri 10am-2am, Sat 10:30am-2am, Sun 10:30am-6pm, cocktails from £8.50, Tube King's Cross/St. Pancras

16 Tucked away in a small courtyard is **Bar Pepito.** Come here to drink sherry and eat tapas in a charming interior with colorful tiles and Spanish decorations. The restaurant may be small, but the good energy here is abundant.
3 Varnishers Yard, Regent's Quarter, camino.uk.com/location/bar-pepito, tel. 020 7841 7331, open Mon-Fri 5pm-midnight, Sat 6pm-midnight, tapas from £4, Tube King's Cross

17 **Mildreds** is one of the better vegetarian and vegan restaurants in London. The menu includes dishes such as sweet potato curry and noodles with bok choy, kimchi, and tofu, as well as colorful salads and burgers. They take reservations only for large groups but order a drink at the bar and a table will be ready before you know it.
200 Pentonville Road, www.mildreds.co.uk, tel. 020 7278 9422, open Sun 10am-10pm, Mon-Fri noon-11pm, Sat 10am-11pm, mains from £12, Tube King's Cross

23 As the name suggests, at **The Elk in the Woods** you'll feel as if you were in a forest cabin somewhere. The interior is full of wood, deer antlers, and animal skins. Come here from early in the morning to late in the evening for a sandwich, chicken salad, or steak. Reservations are recommended.
37-39 Camden Passage, www.the-elk-in-the-woods.co.uk, tel. 020 7226 3535, open daily 9am-11pm, from £10, Tube Angel

25 At this nameless bar, known simply as **69 Colebrooke Row,** the cocktails are astonishingly good. This small cocktail bar is tucked away on a calm street, and if you're not paying attention, you'll walk right by it. Inside it feels as if you've stepped into the 1920s, and owner Tony Conigliaro mixes up cocktails with names like Death in Venice, the Honeysuckle, and Spitfire.
69 Colebrooke Row, www.69colebrookerow.com, tel. 075 4052 8593, open Sun-Wed 5pm-midnight, Thur 5pm-1am, Fri-Sat 5pm-2am, from £11, Tube Angel

⚡ **Ottolenghi** is a well-known figure in London and far beyond. His books are best-sellers, and he put ingredients such as pomegranate, tahini, and za'atar on the map. One of his delis and restaurants is on Upper Street, where you can enjoy Mediterranean fare and copious amounts of vegetables. Reservations are advised.

287 Upper Street, www.ottolenghi.co.uk, tel. 020 7288 1454, open Mon-Sat 8am-10:30pm, Sun 9am-7pm, from £10, Tube Angel/Highbury & Islington

③⓪ **Fig & Olive** is popular among hip Islington residents. Locals come here for the ambience, the delicious food, and the excellent service. European food with a Mediterranean twist—such as moussaka, sea bass, and lamb—are served up in a sleek, modern interior. During the day you can come here for breakfast or a light lunch.

151 Upper Street, www.figolive.co.uk, tel. 020 7354 2605, open Mon-Thur 11am-11pm, Fri 11am-11:30pm, Sat 9am-11:30pm, Sun 9am-10:30pm, from £13, Tube Angel/Highbury & Islington

③③ Located in an old building that dates from around 1800, you'll find the charming gastropub **The Pig and Butcher.** The ambience is inviting, the interior is warm and homey, and the food is typically English. The menu consists of local products, such as vegetables and meat sourced from farmers around England. Order lamb, steak, or grilled fish, or do like a local and have a traditional Sunday roast.

80 Liverpool Road, www.thepigandbutcher.co.uk, tel. 020 7226 8304, open Mon-Wed 5pm-11pm, Thur 5pm-midnight, Fri-Sat noon-midnight, Sun noon-9pm, from £15, Tube Angel/Highbury & Islington

SHOPPING

① **Coal Drops Yard** is a brand-new shopping street in the heart of King's Cross that offers retail pleasure as well as plenty of charming places to eat. The industrial buildings date back to 1850 and were originally constructed to store coal, but they have recently been converted. Reopening in October 2018, the

shopping district is now home to stores including Lost Property of London, Manifesto, Cubitts, Cheaney, and Tom Dixon.

King's Cross, www.coaldropsyard.com, open daily, Tube King's Cross

19 Two graphic designers with a love for office supplies are the brains behind **Present & Correct.** This is a shop with a collection of simple yet stylishly designed stationery and office supplies, such as notebooks, paper clips, envelopes, books, prints, and postcards. It's a great spot to pick up some gifts.

23 Arlington Way, www.presentandcorrect.com, tel. 020 7278 2460, open Tue-Sat noon-6:30pm, Tube Angel

21 With the arrival of famous retail chains such as Reiss, **Camden Passage** has significantly changed. However, collectors and antique lovers can still come here every Wednesday and Saturday in search of antique and vintage objects. On other days, you can check out stores such as Annie for vintage clothes or Rockarchive Gallery for prints of rock stars.

Camden Passage, www.camdenpassageislington.co.uk, open market Wed & Sat 9am-6pm, Fri 10am-6pm, Sun 11am-6pm, Tube Angel

22 As a young girl, graphic and interior designer Lizzie Evans shopped in Camden Passage. Today she now has her own store here, called **Smug,** where you'll find furniture from the 1950s, handmade toys, hip kitchen accessories, and ceramics.

13 Camden Passage, www.ifeelsmug.com, tel. 020 7354 0253, open Mon-Tue & Sun noon-5pm, Wed & Fri 11am-6pm, Thur noon-7pm, Sat 10am-6pm, Tube Angel

24 Creative souls will undoubtedly feel like kids in a candy shop at **Cass Art.** Spread out over three floors, the store has everything you could imagine when it comes to painting, drawing, and art supplies. This is a great place to go for artists and students as well as anyone who loves to be creative. There are also regular workshops and readings here.

66-67 Colebrooke Row, www.cassart.co.uk, tel. 020 7354 2999, open Mon-Wed & Fri 9:30am-7pm, Thur 9:30am-8pm, Sat 10am-7pm, Sun noon-6pm, Tube Angel

26 The brand **Aesop** was founded in 1987 and specializes in natural personal care products. Everything has been rigorously tested and is 100 percent natural. The store's minimalist interior—with white walls, wooden floors, and metal shelves—invokes something of a 1930s laboratory.
56 Cross Street, www.aesop.com, tel. 020 3637 6230, open Mon-Sat 10am-6pm, Sun noon-5pm, Tube Angel/Highbury & Islington

28 **Albam** is a must-visit store for the fashion-conscious man. This is where all of London's hipsters shop. The collection is based around trendy street wear, including denim, fine knits, and colorful jackets with nice details.
286 Upper Street, www.albamclothing.com, tel. 020 7354 1424, open Mon-Sat 11am-7pm, Sun 11:30am-5:30pm, Tube Angel/Highbury & Islington

31 **Aria** is a store that sells wonderful items for the home, including designer furniture, great accessories, and one-of-a-kind gift items. Just across the road, on Upper Street, you'll also find Aria One Six Eight (by the same owner). Here, they carry clothing, bags, and other fashion accessories from well-known and lesser-known brands alike, including Issey Miyake, Tom Dixon, and Sarah Straussberg.
Barnsbury Hall, Barnsbury Street, www.ariashop.co.uk, tel. 020 7704 6222, open Sun 11am-5pm, Mon-Sat 10am-6:30pm, Tube Angel/Highbury & Islington

32 At **After Noah** you can find one-of-a-kind gifts. Among the old and antique furniture, the postcards, and the many knickknacks, you'll also find a great collection of old-fashioned toys.
121 Upper Street, www.afternoah.com, tel. 020 7359 4281, open Mon-Sat 10am-6pm, Sun 11am-5pm, Tube Angel/Highbury & Islington

Smug's
TOP TEN
gift ideas

MORE TO EXPLORE

🔟 Behind King's Cross station you'll find **Granary Square,** a new square with spectacular fountains. It's a wonderful spot to hang out on a sunny day. The renovated warehouses are now home to trendy restaurants and the university building of London's most famous fashion school, Central Saint Martins. Events and festivals are organized here year-round, including an open-air movie theater in the summer and an ice-skating rink in the winter.

Granary Square, www.kingscross.co.uk/granary-square, Tube King's Cross

🔞 For classical music, art, and theater, head to **Kings Place.** This cultural center has two concert halls, several art galleries, a bar, and the restaurant Rotunda. Come here during the day or at night for a bite to eat or to sit outside and enjoy a drink with a view of the canal.

90 York Way, www.kingsplace.co.uk, tel. 020 7520 1490, open daily, tickets start at £10, Tube King's Cross

18 The **Old Red Lion Theater** is an intimate, charming theater with just sixty seats and a typical English ambience. For more than thirty years, new and classic theater productions have been performed here. If you want to hang out a little while after a performance, head to the Old Red Lion Pub for an English beer or a glass of wine.
418 St John Street, www.oldredliontheatre.co.uk, tel. 033 3012 4963, open daily, Tube Angel

20 With more than 300 years' history, **Sadler's Wells** is the dance theater of London. All forms of dance can be seen here, from modern and tango to hip-hop and flamenco. This is highly recommended for those who enjoy contemporary dance.
Rosebery Avenue, www.sadlerswells.com, tel. 020 7863 8000, open daily, Tube Angel

29 For a pleasant, intimate evening out, **Almeida Theatre** is the perfect place for theater lovers. The venue stages primarily original, international productions performed by both rising stars and well-known actors. Next door to the theater is the Almeida Café Bar, where you can stop for a bite to eat before or after the show. The menu features mostly classic British fare, and there is also a special theater menu.
Almeida Street, www.almeida.co.uk, tel. 020 7359 4404, open Mon-Sat 10am-11:30pm, Tube Angel/Highbury & Islington

34 For a great night of film head to **Screen on the Green.** Watch a film in this small, charming theater from the comfort of a nice armchair or loveseat. Here they show everything from blockbuster hits to old classics.
83 Upper Street, www.everymancinema.com/screen-on-the-green, tel. 087 1906 9060, open daily, tickets start at £12, Tube Angel

MARYLEBONE, REGENT'S PARK & PRIMROSE HILL

ABOUT THE WALK

The walk begins in the charming Marylebone. On Marylebone High Street you'll find a selection of fantastic stores and restaurants. The second part of the walk will take you to Regent's Park and Primrose Hill, which are great places to get some fresh air, either on foot or by bike. This is a long, varied route that lets you see two very nice neighborhoods in London.

THE NEIGHBORHOODS

Marylebone and Primrose Hill are two charming neighborhoods with a small-town feel. In between you'll find Regent's Park.

Marylebone is located north of Oxford Street and is primarily home to well-heeled professionals, expats, and famous people. This neighborhood has a nice small-town feel but with a selection of stores and restaurants that make it the envy of all others. Marylebone High Street and Marylebone Lane form the central axis of this neighborhood. In the 1960s, this area was a favorite of the Beatles, and both Paul McCartney and John Lennon have lived here. Other famous former residents include Charles Dickens, Jimi Hendrix, and fictional detective Sherlock Holmes.

North of Marylebone is **Regent's Park,** a beautiful park surrounded by stately buildings. From the top of **Primrose Hill,** the view out over the city is spectacular. Primrose Hill is also the name of the nearby residential neighborhood. It is a charming, hidden corner of London. The small-town feel, colorful facades, and seagulls overhead give it a laid-back atmosphere. The neighborhood is formed around Regent's Park Road. On this street there are many nice stores and a variety of amazing restaurants. The odds are good you'll see a familiar face here because the neighborhood also has its share of famous residents. In the 1990s the area was home to the Primrose Hill set, London's hippest group of friends, including Kate Moss, Jude Law, and Ewan McGregor.

SHORT ON TIME? HERE ARE THE HIGHLIGHTS:

③ ST. CHRISTOPHER'S PLACE + ⑨ THE GOLDEN HIND + ⑳ ALFIES ANTIQUE MARKET + ㉒ REGENT'S PARK + ㉖ PRIMROSE HILL

£35.00

TIPS

// A long, varied walk—
great for first-time visitors
// A perfect walk
for shopaholics
// The second half of this
walk is well-suited
for biking

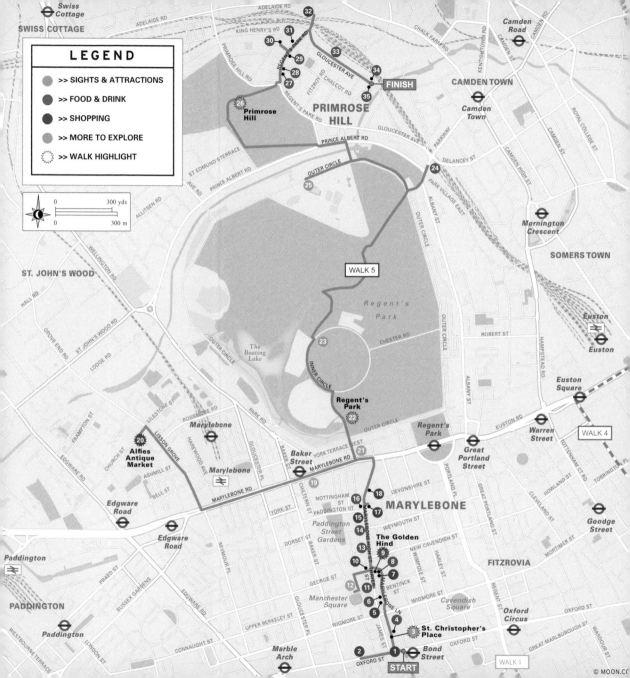

WALK 5 DESCRIPTION (approx. 6.5 mi/10.5 km)

When you exit the Bond Street Tube station, you'll find yourself in the middle of the bustling shopping street Oxford Street ❶. To the left is Selfridges ❷. From there, walk back toward the station and turn left down the alleyway next to H&M, which will take you to St. Christopher's Place ❸ ❹, where you'll start to leave the shopping masses behind you. From here, continue on the street also called St. Christopher's Place. This will take you to Wigmore Street. Cross the street and head down Marylebone Lane ❺ ❻ ❼ ❽ ❾. At the end you'll reach Thayer Street. Cross the street and continue down George Street ❿, or turn left for Peruvian food ⓫. To check out the Wallace Collection ⓬, continue on George Street, then turn left on Spanish Place toward Manchester Square. Not in the mood for art? Then bear right on Thayer Street, which leads onto Marylebone High Street. This street offers hours of shopping fun and plenty of great places to reload ⓭ ⓮ ⓯ ⓰ ⓱. At the end of Marylebone High Street and just past the Conran Shop ⓲, you'll come to Marylebone Road. Head left a short distance for Ambika P3 ⓳. Those interested in antiques will want to take a bit of a detour here and continue on Marylebone Road, then go right on Lissen Grove and turn down the fifth street on the left, Church Street. Tucked away behind the market stalls you'll find the enormous building that houses Alfies Antique Market ⓴. If you'd rather skip Alfies, cross Marylebone Road to the Royal Academy of Music ㉑. Directly behind this is the entrance to Regent's Park ㉒. Within the Inner Circle you'll find Queen Mary's Gardens and the Open Air Theatre ㉓. For a delicious lunch, exit the park up and to the right and take Gloucester Gate to York & Albany ㉔. Take Gloucester Gate back to the park and turn right on the Outer Circle to the London Zoo ㉕. Walk back a bit and go left across St. Mark's Square to Prince Albert Road. Turn left and enter Primrose Hill park ㉖ for a phenomenal view of the city. Exit the park to the north, and on Regent's Park Road you'll find a variety of great restaurants ㉗ ㉘ ㉙ ㉚ ㉛ and shops ㉜. At the end of the street, turn right on Gloucester Avenue for even more nice spots to shop and eat ㉝ ㉞ ㉟. From here you can walk along the canal to Camden.

SIGHTS & ATTRACTIONS

12 **The Wallace Collection** is not well known among the general public, which makes it all that much nicer. It is an impressive collection of 17th-century paintings, 18th-century furniture, and a variety of other art objects. Everything is exhibited in the intimate setting of the stately home where the objects have always been. The sunny courtyard is also a unique setting for a delicious afternoon tea.
Manchester Square, www.wallacecollection.org, tel. 020 7563 9500, open daily 10am-5pm, free, Tube Bond Street/Baker Street

19 Directly across from the famous Madame Tussauds is the gigantic underground hangar **Ambika P3.** Come here to see all types of artwork, from installations to photography—all of which are perfectly suited for exhibition in this enormous space.
University of Westminster, 35 Marylebone Road, www.p3exhibitions.com, tel. 020 7911 5876, open Mon-Fri 8am-6:30pm, Sat 8am-1pm, free, Tube Baker Street

21 The museum at **The Royal Academy of Music** is a true pleasure for music lovers. The instruments, art objects, and sheet music on display are all still actively used by staff and students at the academy. If you're lucky, perhaps there will be an impromptu concert while you're there.
Marylebone Road, www.ram.ac.uk, tel. 020 7873 7373, open Mon-Fri 11:30am-5:30pm, Sat noon-4pm, free, Tube Baker Street/Regent's Park

FOOD & DRINK

4 For a good cup of coffee, Londoners head to **Workshop Coffee,** and you know it's always good where the locals go. A team of hip baristas here roast the coffee themselves. To go with your coffee, there is also an assortment of sandwiches, croissants, and cakes.
1 Barrett Street, www.workshopcoffee.com, tel. 020 7251 6501, open Mon-Fri 7am-7pm, Sat-Sun 9am-6pm, from £3, Tube Bond Street

6 **Paul Rothe & Son,** established in 1900, is still run by the same family. This typically English and deliciously old-fashioned deli/restaurant is the perfect place to come for a tasty sandwich and a simple cup of tea.

35 Marylebone Lane, tel. 020 7935 6783, open Mon-Fri 8am-6pm, Sat 11:30am-5pm, from £3.50, Tube Bond Street

8 Looking for a place to indulge in some delicious, clean eating? Then head to **The Good Life Eatery** for some fresh-pressed juice and a superfood salad. Here the health conscious can kickstart their day with an ultra-nutritious breakfast—choose from items such as spelt quinoa scones, gluten-free oats, homemade granola, poached eggs, blueberries, berry and chia compote, and almond butter. Anyone hankering for a traditional English breakfast is probably better off going somewhere else.

69 Marylebone Lane, www.goodlifeeatery.com, tel. 020 7487 5359, open Sun 9am-6pm, Mon-Fri 8am-9pm, Sat 9am-7pm, breakfast £7, Tube Bond Street

9 A trip to London is, of course, not complete without fish and chips, and you'd be hard pressed to find anywhere that makes them better than at the **Golden Hind.** This unassuming café has been around since 1914 and is still as popular as ever.

73 Marylebone Lane, www.goldenhindrestaurant.com, tel. 020 7486 3644, open Mon-Fri noon-3pm & 6pm-10pm, Sat 6pm-10pm, from £7, Tube Bond Street

11 Hidden away in a charming, somewhat secluded space with a cozy interior lies **Pachamama.** This restaurant serves up refined Peruvian cuisine made with locally sourced products. The dishes are meant for sharing and include delicacies such as sea bass ceviche with tiger's milk, super spicy Peruvian fried chicken, and plantains with *yacón* syrup. To go with your meal, order a cocktail with pisco. Everything is delicious! They also have vegetarian and gluten-free options.

18 Thayer Street, www.pachamamalondon.com, tel. 020 7935 9393, open Sun 11am-4pm & 6pm-10pm, Mon-Fri noon-3pm & 6pm-11pm, Sat 11am-4pm & 6pm-11pm, mains from £15, Tube Bond Street

WALK 5 > MARYLEBONE, REGENT'S PARK & PRIMROSE HILL

⓭ The Providores & Tapa Room is a long-running hit. It is always busy at the Tapa Room, but the wait for the sensational Asian-Australian food is more than worth it. Upstairs in the restaurant Providores, they serve up more complex meals, which makes it the perfect place for a special occasion.

109 Marylebone High Street, www.theprovidores.co.uk, tel. 020 7935 6175, open Sun 9am-3pm & 4pm-10pm, Mon-Fri 8am-10:30pm, Sat 9am-3pm & 4pm-10:30pm, two-course meal £35, Tube Baker Street/Bond Street

⓮ There are a limited number of tables at the cheese shop and deli **La Fromagerie.** If you manage to get one, there are a variety of delicious dishes to choose from on the day's menu. Of course, the cheese platter is always an excellent option.

2-6 Moxon Street, www.lafromagerie.co.uk, tel. 020 7935 0341, open Mon-Fri 8am-7:30pm, Sat 9am-7pm, Sun 10am-6pm, from £9.80, Tube Baker Street/Bond Street

⓰ The Natural Kitchen is a grocery store where everything is fresh, seasonal, organic, or handmade. You'll also find superfoods and gluten-free products. You can come here any time of day for a bite to eat or something to drink. If there's no place to sit in front, there are more tables in the back. There is also a café upstairs.

77-78 Marylebone High Street, www.thenaturalkitchen.com, tel. 020 7935 8151, open Mon-Fri 7am-6pm, Sat-Sun 9am-5pm, from £7.95, Tube Baker Street

㉔ In the Gordon Ramsay bar at the **York & Albany** hotel you can eat fresh brick-oven pizza and sip cocktails, beer, or a good glass of wine. If you'd prefer a more extensive dinner, you can also order off the menu from the hotel's restaurant.

127-129 Parkway, www.gordonramsayrestaurants.com/york-and-albany, tel. 020 7387 5700, open Mon-Thur 7am-midnight, Fri-Sat 7am-1am, Sun 7am-11pm, from £19, Tube Camden Town/Mornington Crescent

㉗ Odette's is a favorite spot among romantic locals. Both the restaurant and the bar are incredibly charming, and the modern British dishes go beyond your everyday fare. One taste and you'll understand why Chef Bryn Williams was

GF V – £ 4.50

TERIYAKI SALMON FILLET
GF DF – £ 6.75 **8**

DAILY SOUP
(always vegan and
gluten free)
choice of toast V
£ 6.50

SMOKED SALMON
£ 4.00

EM & KALE
SIDE SALAD
/ dijon vinaigrette
GF DF – £ 4.00

SHREDDED SEASONAL
GREENS W/ OMEGA
SEEDS GF DF – £ 2.50

£4.50

THE
GOOD
LIFE

selected to prepare a birthday banquet for Queen Elizabeth. This is a great spot for a special dinner, but be sure to reserve a table in advance.

130 Regent's Park Road, NW1, www.odettesprimrosehill.com, tel. 020 7586 8569, open Tue-Fri noon-2:30pm & 6pm-10pm, Sat noon-3pm & 6pm-10pm, Sun noon-3pm, from £25, Tube Chalk Farm

28 If you've got a penchant for desserts, take note. **Sweet Things** sells the best cakes, brownies, and cupcakes in London. This store/café has won various prizes, and the fudgy chocolate brownies are fabulous.

138 Regent's Park Road, www.sweetthings.biz, tel. 020 7722 2107, open Mon-Fri 8:30am-5pm, Sat-Sun 9:30am-6pm, Tube Chalk Farm

29 **Lemonia** is a charming restaurant that serves Greek fare. It is very popular among the locals. If you can't choose, then opt for the *mezze*, and they'll fill your table with a variety of tasty bites.

89 Regent's Park Road, www.lemonia.co.uk, tel. 020 7586 7454, open Mon-Sat noon-3pm & 6pm-11pm, Sun noon-3:30pm, set meal £25, Tube Chalk Farm

30 Vegetarians are all too often stuck choosing between one or two measly menu options, but not at **Manna.** The menu here offers only delicious, creative vegetarian dishes. This is also a great choice for non-vegetarians who are okay to forgo meat for a meal.

4 Erskine Road, www.mannav.com, tel. 020 7722 8028, open Tue-Fri noon-3pm & 6:30pm-10pm, Sat noon-3pm & 6pm-10pm, Sun noon-7:30pm, from £15, Tube Chalk Farm

31 **Greenberry Café** is a charming neighborhood restaurant where you can come for a cup of coffee or a good glass of wine as well as a quick bite or an extensive meal. They serve up dishes such as mushroom risotto and chicken breast with Greek yogurt and flatbread. At lunchtime, the restaurant is usually hopping with local residents, business owners, and posh moms. When it's really busy, they are not likely to seat you if you're having only a drink.

101 Regent's Park Road, www.greenberrycafe.co.uk, tel. 020 7483 3765, open Mon 9am-3pm, Tue-Sat 9am-10pm, Sun 9am-3pm, from £15, Tube Chalk Farm

③③ The Lansdowne is a shabby-chic restaurant that is very popular among the local posh moms and their kids. Come here for quiche with onions, endive and goat cheese, or steak with fries. Regardless of what you order, you're certain to enjoy the laid-back atmosphere. For kids, there are also pizzas on the menu.

90 Gloucester Avenue, www.thelansdownepub.co.uk, tel. 020 7483 0409, open Mon-Sat noon-11pm, Sun noon-10:30pm, from £16, Tube Chalk Farm

③④ Melrose & Morgan is a deli where you'll be tempted to buy all types of jars and packages of yummy treats that you didn't even know you needed. In the café, you can also order a delicious breakfast or lunch.

42 Gloucester Avenue, www.melroseandmorgan.com, tel. 020 7722 0011, open Mon-Fri 8am-7pm, Sat 8am-6pm, Sun 9am-5pm, from £6, Tube Chalk Farm

③⑤ The Engineer is the starting point for your perfect boozy Sunday. Do as the locals do and order a beer and a Sunday roast, and then settle down by the fire to enjoy a laid-back afternoon. There are often sports games on the TV, and when the sun is shining, the beer garden is an excellent place to sit back and relax.

65 Gloucester Avenue, www.theengineerprimrosehill.co.uk, tel. 020 7483 1890, open Sun noon-10:30pm, Mon-Sat noon-11pm, Sunday roast £17, Tube Chalk Farm

SHOPPING

❶ The largest and undoubtedly busiest shopping street in all of Europe is **Oxford Street.** Every main retail outlet has a store here. You'll find TopShop, H&M, Gap, Zara, Urban Outfitters, Primark, River Island, Uniqlo, and Marks & Spencer—all conveniently right next to each other.

Oxford Street, www.oxfordstreet.co.uk, open Mon-Sat 9:30am-9pm, Sun 11:30am-6pm, Tube Marble Arch/Bond Street/Oxford Circus

❷ There are a variety of department stores on Oxford Street, but **Selfridges** is a favorite among Londoners. Come here for food, designer clothes, shoes, make-up, gadgets, home accessories, and much more. Among all of the beautiful objects for sale you'll also find a variety of restaurants and cafés.
400 Oxford Street, www.selfridges.com, open Mon-Sat 9:30am-9pm, Sun 11:30am-6pm, Tube Bond Street/Marble Arch

❺ **Tracey Neuls** uses old-fashioned techniques to turn simple women's shoes into ultra-modern works of art in a way that is timeless rather than trendy. Inside, the store is truly exceptional, and the shoe displays are very imaginative.
29 Marylebone Lane, www.traceyneuls.com, tel. 020 7935 0039, open Mon-Fri 11am-6:30pm, Sat noon-6pm, Sun noon-5pm, Tube Bond Street

❼ **Content Beauty/Wellbeing** is filled top to bottom with high-end, natural, personal care products you won't find just anywhere else. Downstairs you can also treat yourself to a facial, makeover, or massage.
14 Bulstrode Street, www.beingcontent.com, tel. 020 3075 1006, open Mon-Fri 10am-7pm, Sat 10am-6pm, Tube Bond Street

❿ The founder of the magazine *Wallpaper* is also behind the magazine and eponymous store **Monocle.** In this tiny shop you'll find accessories, books, clothes, fragrances, and other beautiful objects from big names such as Comme des Garçons, A Kind of Guise, and Delfonics—all of which have been specially designed for Monocle.
2a George Street, www.monocle.com, tel. 020 7486 8770, open Mon-Sat 11am-7pm, Sun noon-6pm, Tube Bond Street

⓯ It is worth a trip to **Daunt Books** if for nothing else than to check out the amazing historical building and take in the great atmosphere. The store has an excellent collection of travel books.
83 Marylebone High Street, www.dauntbooks.co.uk, tel. 020 7224 2295, open Mon-Sat 9am-7:30pm, Sun 11am-6pm, Tube Baker Street/Bond Street

17 For a wonderful fragrance, go to **Le Labo.** The perfumes are mixed right here in the store. The fragrances are set, but the ingredients are mixed together on the spot, which means you always have a fresh perfume. You can choose from natural scents such as jasmine, patchouli, fig, and musk. The oils, creams, and scented candles also smell divine.

28a Devonshire Street, www.lelabofragrances.com, tel. 020 3441 1535, open Mon-Wed & Fri-Sat 10am-6:30pm, Thur 10am-7pm, Sun noon-5pm, Tube Baker Street

18 For stylish furniture, kitchen accessories, and glasswork, the **Conran Shop** is an absolute must. You'll have to try really hard to leave the store empty-handed. Downstairs you'll find the Conran Kitchen, where you can get a nice cup of coffee and a sandwich or a yummy piece of cake.

55 Marylebone High Street, www.theconranshop.co.uk, tel. 020 7723 2223, open Mon-Sat 10am-7pm, Sun 11:30am-6pm, Tube Baker Street

20 To get to **Alfies Antique Market,** you'll have to deviate from the designated walking route. This is a true treasure trove for anyone who loves antiques and vintage items. In this enormous covered labyrinth more than one hundred venders sell their wares, from teaspoons to sideboards. Tin Tin Collectables is a great spot for vintage clothing, and model Kate Moss is regularly spotted here. At the Rooftop Kitchen you can also get a classic English breakfast or lunch.

13-25 Church Street, www.alfiesantiques.com, tel. 020 7723 6066, open Tue-Sat 10am-6pm, Tube Edgware Road/Marylebone

32 **Tann Rokka** offers an extraordinary collection of extravagant antiques, modern accessories, furniture, and other items for the home. This is always a great place to come and look around.

123 Regent's Park Road, www.tannrokka.com, tel. 020 7722 3999, open Mon-Thur by appointment, Fri-Sun 10am-6pm, Tube Chalk Farm

MORE TO EXPLORE

3 Escape the shopping masses on Oxford Street and discover **St. Christopher's Place.** On this charming square and street you'll find a mix of one-of-a-kind stores, cafés, and restaurants.

For handmade hats, check out Christys', and pop into Euphorium for coffee and pastries. In addition to the small, independent stores, around the corner you'll find a number of big British fashion retailers, including Reiss, Jigsaw, Whistles, and Phase Eight.

St. Christopher's Place, www.stchristophersplace.com, open daily, Tube Bond Street

🔖 The gorgeous **Regent's Park** is someplace you could easily spend the entire day. Surrounded by beautiful stately buildings, the park offers something for everyone, from the Open Air Theatre and the rose gardens to the boat rides and the London Zoo.

Regent's Park, www.royalparks.org.uk/parks/the-regents-park, tel. 030 0061 2300, open daily 5am-9:30pm, Tube Baker Street/Regent's Park/Camden Town

㉓ During the summer season, the **Open Air Theatre** offers a wonderful opportunity to enjoy productions of opera, ballet, and Shakespeare in the park. This landmark theater is a firm fixture of summer in the city, and the shows are considered among London's cultural highlights.

Regent's Park, www.openairtheatre.org, tel. 084 4826 4242, open afternoon and evening shows during the summer, entrance £5-£23, Tube Baker Street/Regent's Park

㉕ If you want to see all of the animals at the **London Zoo,** you'll easily need an entire day. There are more than 12,000 individual animals and more than 700 species here, including in the Gorilla Kingdom and at the Penguin Beach. In the summer, the zoo sometimes organizes late night openings, which include live shows, food, and a silent disco. These evenings are very popular and booking in advance is required.

Regent's Park, www.zsl.org/zsl-london-zoo, tel. 034 4225 1826, open daily except Christmas Day, entrance £29.75, Tube Chalk Farm

🔖 **Primrose Hill** is located at the north edge of Regent's Park and offers a surprisingly wonderful view of London. Up at the top is a sign that explains all the things you see in the distance. This spot has been featured in numerous movies and books, including *Bridget Jones: The Edge of Reason*.

Primrose Hill, www.royalparks.org.uk/parks/the-regents-park, open daily 5am-9:30pm, free, Tube Chalk Farm

KNIGHTSBRIDGE & CHELSEA

ABOUT THE WALK

This walk is long but varied. It takes you past great stores, coffee shops, and restaurants; however, the main focus of this route is art and culture. You'll walk by major museums and famous sights. The first half through Hyde Park, in particular, is perfect for biking.

THE NEIGHBORHOODS

Chelsea and Knightsbridge were once two small, verdant towns located a fair distance from the polluted capital. Today, however, these two up-scale neighborhoods are located in southwest London.

Chelsea was the birthplace of Swinging London back when Mick Jagger and other rock 'n' rollers used to hang out in the hip cafés and boutiques here. **King's Road** was a real-life catwalk where the latest fashion trends were conceived. Today, not much is left of the Swinging Sixties, and Chelsea is synonymous with wealth and excess. Famous people, bankers, traders, and billionaires from around the world live in beautiful, renovated Victorian buildings here.

Knightsbridge is home to London's most expensive homes, and some of the streets have the highest density of millionaires in the world. This is clearly reflected in the selection of stores and restaurants in the area. **Sloane Street** is bursting with incredibly expensive shops from top fashion labels. The famous department stores **Harrods** and **Harvey Nichols** are also located here.

An increasing number of buildings in the area are purchased as investments by wealthy foreigners, primarily from Russia, China, and the Middle East. The result is that many buildings are empty because their owners live abroad. Some neighborhoods are so full of empty buildings that they are known as ghost towns.

There is no shortage of nature and culture in this area. **Hyde Park** is one of London's biggest parks and is a great place to go walking, jogging, or biking. Another reason that this neighborhood is so popular among tourists is the many museums. Three of the best museums in the world can be found here: the **Natural History Museum, Victoria and Albert Museum,** and the **Science Museum.**

SHORT ON TIME? HERE ARE THE HIGHLIGHTS:

1 HYDE PARK + 8 SCIENCE MUSEUM + 10 VICTORIA & ALBERT MUSEUM + 25 DUKE OF YORK SQUARE + 32 HARVEY NICHOLS

TIPS

// Varied walk—great for first-time visitors
// The many museums make this walk a perfect way to take in art and culture
// Also well-suited for biking

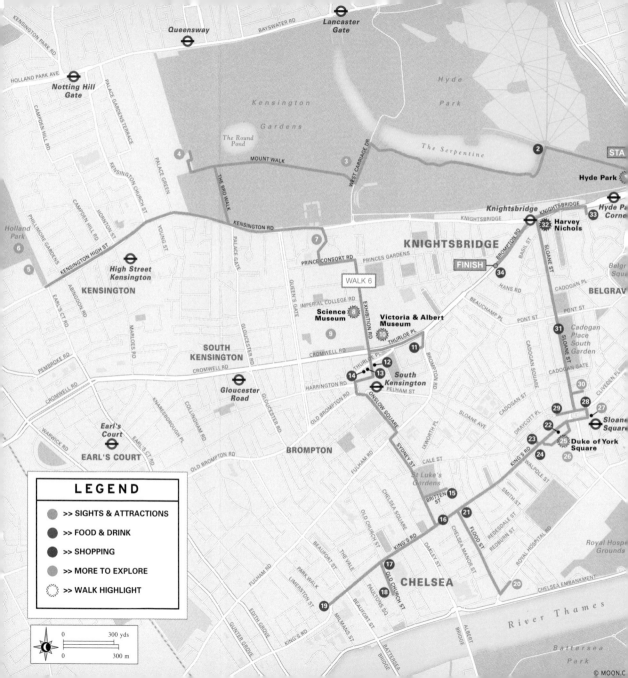

9 You can see dinosaurs, volcanos, fossils, geological artifacts, and a variety of animal exhibitions at the **Natural History Museum.** This museum is located in a large, beautiful building and has wonderful displays. There is especially a lot to see and discover here for children.

Cromwell Road, www.nhm.ac.uk, tel. 020 7942 5000, open daily 10am-5:50pm, free to permanent exhibitions, Tube South Kensington

10 The **Victoria and Albert Museum** is a fantastic museum for everything that has anything to do with art and design in the broadest sense of the word—fashion, architecture, photography, furniture, glass, ceramics, and much more. Items here cover a period of about three thousand years. In addition to the permanent collection, the museum also has excellent temporary exhibitions. Be sure to stop at the museum store and in the courtyard for afternoon tea.

Cromwell Road, www.vam.ac.uk, tel. 020 7942 2000, open Sat-Thur 10am-5:45pm, Fri 10am-10pm, free to permanent collection, Tube South Kensington

26 Crazy about contemporary art? Then you must visit the enormous **Saatchi Gallery,** where you can see regularly changing exhibitions with works by emerging and established artists who have never or not often before been exhibited in the UK.

Duke of York's HQ, King's Road Chelsea, www.saatchi-gallery.co.uk, tel. 020 7811 3085, open daily 10am-6pm, free, Tube Sloane Square

FOOD & DRINK

2 **Serpentine Bar & Kitchen** is a fabulous café on the lake in Hyde Park. This is a great spot to start the day off with a good breakfast. You can also come here at the end of the day to see the sunset, which is particularly romantic.

Serpentine Road, Hyde Park, www.serpentinebarandkitchen.com, tel. 020 7706 8114, open daily 8am-7pm, from £10, Tube Knightsbridge

⑫ London certainly has no shortage of great places to eat, and **Fernandez & Wells** is among the favorites. Order a strong espresso and a freshly made sandwich or settle down in the afternoon for a glass of wine and a well-deserved cheese platter. This is the ideal spot to come after a museum visit.
8 Exhibition Road, www.fernandezandwells.com, tel. 020 7589 7473, open Mon-Sat 8am-11pm, Sun 8am-8pm, sandwich £7.50, Tube South Kensington

⑬ **Comptoir Libanais** is the perfect place to relax after a visit to a museum. This Lebanese restaurant serves up generous dishes of *mezze*, tajines, and tasty wraps with yummy dips. The idea is that everything is for sharing. Be sure to also try the fresh lemonades, such as pomegranate and orange blossom. This is also a great spot for breakfast.
1-5 Exhibition Road, www.lecomptoir.co.uk, tel. 020 7225 5006, open Mon-Sat 8:30am-midnight, Sun 8:30am-10:30pm, from £9, Tube South Kensington

⑭ Matcha, a type of Japanese green tea, is popular among those in the know—not just as a drink but also as an ingredient. Its versatility is perfectly showcased at **Tombo,** where there are a wide range of matcha drinks and desserts, including matcha latte, matcha ice cream, and matcha cheesecake. The menu also includes Japanese dishes such as sushi and donburi rice bowls and Hawaiian-style *poké* bowls. Healthy and delicious! It's a great spot for an afternoon break.
29 Thurloe Place, www.tombocafe.com, tel. 020 7589 0018, open daily 11:30am-9:30pm, mains from £9, Tube South Kensington

⑮ Tucked away down a small street behind King's Road you'll find **The Builders Arms.** This gastropub is an ideal spot to come for a drink and mix with Chelsea locals. You can also come here for lunch—the menu includes typical pub food.
13 Britten Street, www.thebuildersarmschelsea.co.uk, tel. 020 7349 9040, open Mon-Sat 11am-11pm, Sun noon-10:30pm, from £14, Tube South Kensington

⑱ If you're in the mood for a beer, there is no better place to go in the area than the **The Chelsea Pig.** Stay here for dinner, too, if you're so included. The menu includes excellent dishes such as risotto, steak, and grilled sardines.
35 Old Church Street, www.thechelseapig.com, tel. 020 7352 2908, open Mon-Sat noon-11pm, Sun noon-10:30pm, from £15, Tube Sloane Square

⑲ For a super healthy pit stop, head to **Juicebaby.** This juice bar is the perfect place for raw, organic, and cold-pressed juices. Order an açaí bowl or green salad to go with your juice and try a matcha latte too. Everything here is handmade and organic.

398 King's Road, www.juicebaby.co.uk, tel. 020 7351 2230, open Sun 9am-7pm, Mon-Sat 8am-7pm, Tube Sloane Square/South Kensington

㉔ Partridges Food Market is a bustling Saturday market where you can come to sample and buy the best of British and international food. The delicacies on offer include regional cheeses, freshly baked bread, and locally sourced shellfish, as well as Japanese sushi, French crêpes, and olives from Italy. There is something here for everyone. Since its inception in 2005, the market has grown considerably, and now there are more than 70 different food stalls.

Duke of York Square, www.partridges.co.uk/foodmarket, open Sat 10am-4pm, Tube Sloane Square

㉘ Come to **The Botanist** any time of the day—for lunch, afternoon tea, appetizers, dinner, or cocktails. Here it is often just as much about seeing and being seen as it is about the menu. Be sure to take a look at the restaurant's eye-catching, hand-painted glass wall of natural history designs.

7 Sloane Square, www.thebotanistonsloanesquare.com, tel. 020 7730 0077, open Mon-Wed 8am-11:30pm, Thur 8am-midnight, Fri-Sat 9am-1am, Sun 9am-11:30pm, from £20, Tube Sloane Square

㉝ The Berkeley is a gorgeous hotel with a rooftop pool. The designer afternoon tea in the Caramel Room is a delightful surprise. Referred to as "Prêt-à-Portea," afternoon tea here, which involves cakes and cookies in the shape of bags and shoes, changes every six months. It's a fabulous treat for all the fashion lovers among us.

Wilton Place, www.the-berkeley.co.uk, tel. 020 7235 6000, afternoon tea daily 1pm-5:30pm, £52, Tube Knightsbridge/Hyde Park Corner

SHOPPING

⓫ If you love interior design, then you absolutely must stop in at **Mint.** This store has a thoughtful collection of home accessories and furniture from famous names and unknown designers alike, and from affordable to super expensive. One thing's for sure: all items are equally as original.

2 North Terrace, Alexander Square, www.mintshop.co.uk, tel. 020 7225 2228, open Mon-Wed & Fri-Sat 10:30am-6:30pm, Thur 10:30am-7:30pm, Tube South Kensington/Knightsbridge

⓰ In the 1960s, **King's Road** was known as the place to find the coolest fashion trends and the rock stars who sported them. Although these days the mod squad has moved on and the stores are more of the high-street variety, Vivienne Westwood still has a shop on the street where she made a name for herself (World's End, 430 King's Road).

King's Road west from Sloane Street, Tube Sloane Square

⓱ Designers Guild, known for its colorful fabrics, has a beautiful shop that displays the entire collection. Here you'll find furniture, towels, linens, dinnerware, pillows, wallpaper, and hundreds of fabrics—so many beautiful things, it's difficult to choose.

267-277 King's Road, www.designersguild.com, tel. 020 7351 5775, open Mon-Sat 10am-6pm, Sun noon-5pm (fabric store closed on Sunday), Tube South Kensington/Sloane Square

㉑ Popular in the United States, **Anthropologie** has crossed the pond and now has locations in the UK. The store on King's Road was one of the first European locations and was welcomed by Londoners with great enthusiasm. The beautiful building, which previously housed an antique dealer, offers a unique collection of women's clothes, accessories, and objects for the home. The store also has locations on Regent Street and on Marylebone High Street.

131-141 King's Road, www.anthropologie.eu, tel. 020 7349 3110, open Mon-Sat 10am-7pm, Sun 11:30am-6pm, Tube Sloane Square/South Kensington

㉒ Penhaligon's is the place to go for unique, wonderful English perfumes in old-fashion bottles. Here you'll find the favorite fragrance of Winston Churchill, for example, and a number of historical scents that date back to 1927. There is also a nice selection of bath oils, soaps, and other great accessories. This perfume store has retail outlets throughout the city and in some of the higher-end department stores.

132 King's Road, www.penhaligons.com, tel. 020 7823 9733, open Mon-Tue & Thur-Sat 9:30am-6:30pm, Wed 9:30am-7pm, Sun 11:30pm-6:30pm, Tube Sloane Square/South Kensington

㉓ John Sandoe Books is London's number-one independent literary book store. It is the perfect place to just look around at all the stacks of books and is especially good when you need to find that one book you just can't get anywhere else.

10 Blacklands Terrace, www.johnsandoe.com, tel. 020 7589 9473, open Mon-Sat 9:30am-6:30pm, Sun 11am-5pm, Tube Sloane Square

㉙ The White Company is a must for all things bed and bath. Think pajamas, bathrobes, slippers, and bedding, as well as personal care products, home accessories, clothing, and toys for the little ones.

12 Marylebone High Street, www.thewhitecompany.com, tel. 020 8166 0199, open Mon-Sat 10am-6:30pm, Sun noon-6pm, Tube Baker Street/Bond Street

㉛ Sloane Street is a super expensive shopping street, with high-end stores such as Chloé, Cartier, Gucci, Louis Vuitton, Chanel, and Valentino. If these brands are what you are looking for, you should also check out Old and New Bond Street.

Sloane Street, www.sloane-street.co.uk, open Mon-Sat 10am-6pm, Tube Knightsbridge/Sloane Square

㉜ The fashion-conscious shop at **Harvey Nichols,** where there is a nice collection of all the best-known, exclusive fashion labels. The fifth floor is entirely dedicated to food and has a deli, restaurants, and a great terrace.

109-125 Knightsbridge, www.harveynichols.com, tel. 020 7235 5000, open Mon-Fri 10am-8pm, Sun 11:30am-6pm, Tube Knightsbridge

34 London's best-known shopping attraction is hands down the large department store **Harrods.** It is perhaps best known for its deli, but it is, of course, also known for more than just good food. Harrods has a wonderful selection of high-end items, including everything from clothing, bags, and cosmetics to toys, furniture, and much more. You're likely to find more tourists than Londoners here. The store's large, extravagant Christmas department is typically British, and beginning every August you shop to your heart's content for Christmas tree ornaments and other holiday items.

87-135 Brompton Road, www.harrods.com, tel. 020 7730 1234, open Mon-Sat 10am-9pm, Sun 11:30am-6pm, Tube Knightsbridge

MORE TO EXPLORE

Hyde Park is an enormous green space that is perfect for skating, biking, horseback riding, walking, and picnicking. You can also rent one of the many deck chairs here and just relax. In the middle of the park is the Serpentine lake, which is full of swans, ducks, and other waterbirds and where you can swim or rent a rowboat. Since 1872, the northeast side of Hyde Park, known as the Speakers' Corner, has been a place where people can get on their soapboxes and speak their minds. Anything goes and everything does, which sometimes leads to some funny scenes. If you're with your kids, be sure not to miss the Diana, Princess of Wales Memorial Playground, located in the northwest corner of the park. It is a giant playground, complete with a pirate ship and tepees.

Hyde Park, www.royalparks.org.uk/parks/hyde-park, tel. 020 7298 2100, open 5am-midnight, free, Tube Hyde Park Corner/Knightsbridge

6 Holland Park is a delightful place to escape to when you need a breather from the city's hustle and bustle. The Kyoto Garden—a Japanese garden with a koi pond and waterfall—is located here. In the summer, operas and concerts are held in the park, too. For something to drink, a bite to eat, or even afternoon tea, head to the Belvedere or Holland Park Café.

Ilchester Place, www.rbkc.gov.uk/leisure-and-culture/parks/holland-park, open daily, Tube Holland Park

7 At the impressive **Royal Albert Hall** you can see all types of concerts and ballet performances. The annual series of classical concerts, the "Proms," is very popular, so be sure to book your tickets well in advance.
Kensington Gore, www.royalalberthall.com, tel. 020 7589 8212, opening times and prices vary based on concert/performance, Tube South Kensington

20 The **Chelsea Physic Garden** has been around since 1673, but the medicinal and rare plants still flourish here. This secret spot is the perfect place to escape from the commotion of the big city. In the Tangerine Dream Café you can get a drink or a small bite to eat, and this is an especially good spot for afternoon tea.
66 Royal Hospital Road, www.chelseaphysicgarden.co.uk, tel. 020 7352 5646, open Apr-Oct Mon-Fri 11am-6pm, Nov-Dec & Feb-Mar Mon-Fri & Sun 11am-4pm, entrance £9.50, Tube Sloane Square

25 The pedestrian-only **Duke of York Square** is an unexpected place of calm with an extensive selection of outdoor eating establishments to choose from. There is also great shopping to be done here. Patisserie Valerie is recommended for a sweet fix and Manicomio for a more extensive lunch. The shops include everything from small boutiques to larger stores. Taschen is great for beautiful books, Trilogy for hip jeans, and Space NK Apothecary for beauty products.
Duke of York Square, www.dukeofyorksquare.com, open daily, Tube Sloane Square

27 **Royal Court Theatre** is known for its top-quality performances that always get people talking. New writers and plays are given a great platform here. Theater aficionados should check the website to see what is playing.
Sloane Square, www.royalcourttheatre.com, tel. 020 7565 5000, open daily, tickets start at £12, Mondays £10, Tube Sloane Square

30 At the **Cadogan Hall** concert hall, more than 300 concerts and events are held annually. This primarily includes classical music concerts, including the BBC "Proms." The space is also the home base of the Royal Philharmonic Orchestra.
5 Sloane Terrace, www.cadoganhall.com, tel. 020 7730 4500, opening times vary, Tube Sloane Square

WITH MORE TIME

The routes in this book will take you to most of the city's main highlights. Of course, there are still a number of places worth visiting and things worth seeing that are not included in these walks. We have listed them below. Note that not all of these places are easily accessible by foot from the city, but you can get to them by public transportation.

Ⓐ If you're interested in all things that bloom and blossom, **Kew Gardens** is someplace you won't want to miss. The botanic gardens have been around for more than 200 years and are located a short distance from the city. Plan a full day for your visit because this is the largest collection of living plants in the world. On rainy days, head to the Palm House—an indoor rainforest. If time permits, be sure to also check out the surrounding town of Richmond.
Kew, Richmond, www.kew.org, tel. 020 8332 5655, open daily 10am-6pm, entrance £16, Tube or Train Kew Gardens

Ⓑ **Covent Garden** is known as the entertainment center of London. The area is characterized by its many tourists and street performers. Performers must audition to be able to perform here, so you can expect a good show. You'll also find dozens of places to stop for something to eat or drink, lots of theaters, and the wonderful London Transport Museum, not to mention the myriad shopping opportunities. There are many stores, so start at the Covent Garden Piazza and use that as your orientation point. You'll find clothes on Floral Street, younger crowds are sure to find something they like on Neal Street, and vegetarians will feel right at home on Neal's Yard.
Covent Garden, www.coventgardenlondonuk.com, Tube Covent Garden

Ⓒ Since the release of the movie with the same name, **Notting Hill** has been more popular than ever. Don't come here for culture; come to enjoy the great atmosphere. The neighborhood is full of charming shops and restaurants, such as on Westbourne Grove. Be sure to also check out the **Portobello Road Market.** You won't find any bargains here, but it's something unique to experience. Every day there are different goods on offer, and antiques are only

available on Saturday when the market is at its biggest. The farther down the street you go, the more unique the offerings, so don't be put off by the somewhat shabby overpass.

Portobello Road, W11, www.thehill.co.uk, market open Mon-Wed & Sat 8am-6:30pm, Thur 8am-1pm, Tube Notting Hill Gate/Ladbroke Grove

Ⓓ Londoners come to **Greenwich** to escape downtown London. It's right on the Thames and feels almost like a seaside town. Come here by boat to really get in the right mood for your visit. Once back on land you can stroll through the markets and stop for a bite in any of the charming restaurants. Greenwich's historic center has been declared a World Heritage Site and abounds with culture. There are numerous beautiful old buildings in the picturesque Greenwich Park, starting with the Royal Observatory where you'll find the Prime Meridian. The Maritime Museum, *Cutty Sark*, and the Old Royal Naval College are also definitely worth a visit. The Emirates Air Line is good fun, too, and in five minutes the cable car can shuttle you between the O2 Arena on the Greenwich Peninsula and the Royal Docks. The view, as it takes you over the Thames, is amazing.

Greenwich, www.visitgreenwich.org.uk, DLR Greenwich

(E) If you're in the mood for some fresh air, head to **Hampstead Heath.** This nature reserve in the north of London contains numerous ponds, hills, parks, and woods. Londoners like to come here to go walking and jogging and to enjoy the breathtaking view of the city. Hampstead Village nearby is a charming neighborhood with a small-town feel and lots of great places for shopping, eating, and getting a drink.

Hampstead Heath, www.hampsteadheath.net, Tube Hampstead

(F) For a spectacular view of London, a visit to **The Shard** is highly recommended. Although opinions may be split on the esthetic qualities of Western Europe's tallest building, when it comes to the view from the top everyone agrees it is absolutely amazing. A high-speed elevator brings you up to the top of the building, and from the 69th floor and a height of 800 feet you look out over all of London. The Shard is home to the exclusive Shangri-La Hotel and a variety of great restaurants.

32 London Bridge Street, www.theviewfromtheshard.com, tel. 034 4499 7222, open Sun-Wed 10am-7pm, Thur-Sat 10am-10pm, entrance £25.95, Tube London Bridge

(G) At Warner Bros. Studios, Harry Potter fans can get a behind-the-scenes look at the making of the movies with the **Harry Potter Studio Tour.** See the costumes, props, and sets used in filming, including Hagrid's hut and Diagon Alley, and learn about the various special effects used too. The tour lets you discover the magic behind the movies. The studios are in Watford, which is about 20 miles outside central London, but the train ride out there is well worth it. Make sure to buy your tickets in advance, or you won't get in.

Studio Tour Drive, Leavesden, www.wbstudiotour.co.uk, tel. 020 7323 8299, open daily from 10am, tickets £33, Train Watford Junction

(H) **Broadway Market** is the perfect place to come on a Saturday morning and sit with a cup of coffee while you watch London's trendsetters pass by. Enjoy old-fashioned jellied eel at F. Cooke. Donlon Books and Artwords sell exclusive photography and art books you won't find anywhere else. The stall Spinach & Agushi has the perfect chicken with peanut sauce. And if you already have enough clothing, handmade quilts, knickknacks, and other odds and ends, then head to Off Broadway for a cocktail. Mix with London's hippest at this market.

Broadway Market, www.broadwaymarket.co.uk, open Sat 9am-5pm, Tube Bethnal Green, Train London Fields

(I) After the London 2012 Summer Olympics, the Olympic Park in Stratford was transformed into the **Queen Elizabeth Olympic Park.** It is one of London's largest green spaces, and there's always something going on here. Visit the stadium and other sports facilities where the Games were held. The park also has a variety of cafés and is home to the ArcelorMittal Orbit, an observation tower that offers a great view of the park and city. If you're up for the thrill, you can also slide back down on the world's highest and longest slide at 584 feet (178 meters).

Stratford, www.queenelizabetholympicpark.co.uk, open daily, Tube Stratford

(J) **Hayward Gallery** is a great place to check out innovative modern art. The exhibitions here are unique and thought-provoking and showcase the work of both well-known and lesser-known artists alike. The gallery opened in 1968 and is located close to the Thames. Avoid the crowds by buying your tickets in advance.

Southbank, www.southbankcentre.co.uk/venues/hayward-gallery, tel. 020 7960 4200, open Mon, Wed & Fri-Sun 11am-7pm, Thur 11am-9pm, entrance £15, Tube Waterloo

(K) If you're lucky enough to get tickets for a show at the **National Theatre,** you're in for a guaranteed great night out. Both large- and small-scale productions are presented here, and all are equally impressive. The theater is located in a large concrete building in the South Bank Centre on the Thames

and has three auditoriums, various restaurants and bars, and exhibition spaces. For a peek behind the scenes, be sure to book a backstage tour.

Southbank, www.nationaltheatre.org.uk, tel. 020 7452 3000, open Mon-Sat 9:30am-11pm, Sun noon-6pm, price varies by production, Tube Waterloo

NIGHTLIFE

When it comes to nightlife, London is hands down the number-one city in Europe. Music, movies, theater, comedy, opera, cabaret, dance, etc.—you name it, London's got it.

Soho is London's best-known area for going out. The neighborhood has a plethora of amazing restaurants and charming pubs, along with plenty of theaters, cocktail bars, and nightclubs. Anything is possible here and everything goes. Feeling like a night at the theater? Then head to Soho Theatre or the

National Theatre. Tickets can be hard to come by, however, so always try to book them in advance.

Other parts of the city that are nice to go for a night of dancing or a good drink are Shoreditch and Dalston. Here there are plenty of hot clubs and cocktail bars to choose from.

HOTELS

A good bed, a tasty breakfast, and a nice interior are all key ingredients for a pleasant hotel stay. However, location is perhaps most important of all. A hotel is only really good if you can walk straight out of the lobby and into the bustling city.

Spending the night in central London can be pricy, but there are number of good options, such as the Tommyfield Hotel in Kennington. For those with a roomier budget, there's also the Great Northern Hotel and the Soho Hotel. Want to be able to roll out of a club and right into bed? Then consider a room at the Hoxton or the Ace Hotel in Shoreditch. If you'd rather wake up someplace calmer, you'd probably prefer to stay in a neighborhood such as Greenwich or Richmond.

INDEX

✳ INDEX

MOON
LONDON WALKS
SECOND EDITION

AVALON TRAVEL
Hachette Book Group
1700 Fourth Street
Berkeley, CA 94710, USA
www.moon.com

ISBN 978-1-64049-778-8
Concept & Original Publication
"time to momo London"
© 2019 by mo'media.
All rights reserved.

time to momo

MO' MEDIA
Text and Walks
Kim Snijders

Translation
Eileen Holland

Design
Studio 100% &
Oranje Vormgevers

Photography
Marjolein den Hartog,
Vincent van den Hoogen

Project Editor
Sophie Kreuze

AVALON TRAVEL
Project Editor
Lori Hobkirk

Copy Editor
Beth Fraser

Proofreader
Sandy Chapman

Cover Design
Faceout Studio, Jeff Miller

Typesetting
Cynthia Young

Printed in China by
RR Donnelley
First US printing,
December 2019

Trips to Remember

ANGKOR WAT

BELIZE

GALÁPAGOS ISLANDS

COSTA RICA

FIJI

JAPAN

MACHU PICCHU

MOROCCO

NEW ZEALAND

PATAGONIA

VIETNAM

Grand Adventure

APPALACHIAN TRAIL

PACIFIC COAST HIGHWAY

USA NATIONAL PARKS

MOON.COM
@MOONGUIDES